# THE COVENTRY WE HAVE LOST

## VOLUME 1

Albert Smith & David Fry

Simanda Press
Berkswell 2009

# CONTENTS

The compilers would welcome comments and further information.
These may be addressed to:
Simanda Press, Albert's Cottage, Meriden Road,
Berkswell, Coventry CV7 7BE
email: d.fry@virgin.net

Printed by Centreprint UK Limited
www.centre-print.co.uk

# INTRODUCTION

In compiling this book the co-authors have two aims. Firstly, to help show with illustrations from early photographic postcards, how much of the original City has been lost, secondly to consider the merits of the changes that have occurred, a recurring theme of debate in the City.

The Coventry of this book starts in 1901, when the population was 69,877, with Earlsdon and the upper part of Stoney Stanton Road having only just been embraced by its boundary. It was to be another twenty seven years before areas such as Foleshill, Wyken, Holbrooks, Longford, Walsgrave, Binley, Willenhall, Tile Hill, Canley, Allesley and Coundon would be brought within the city limits. Much of the development which followed in the newly acquired areas was necessary to accommodate an increase in population eventually to exceed 300,000 in a booming industrial city. However, the development that took place at the same time in the city centre is not so easy to accept. Although it is natural that certain buildings will need to be replaced over the years, where they are of historic interest planners should always be able to justify such a loss. As one of the country's foremost medieval cities it is unfortunate, to say the least, now that Coventry is being promoted as a "City of History" to attract tourists, that so little of historic interest remains to be seen. Although the bombing in the last war is blamed for much of the destruction of the City, in fact most of the disappearance of medieval Coventry occurred outside the 1939-1945 period. "The most appalling piece of municipal vandalism recorded in this book" was how the demolition in 1936 of the medieval heart of the City (to make way for Trinity Street), was a judgement made in a publication of the Historical Association. Many would say that this statement could equally describe subsequent post-war developments. As an illustration, in one street alone, in 1955, sixty five buildings, mainly timber framed, that had survived the war were demolished to make way for the Polytechnic. Now it is estimated that only thirty four buildings erected before 1700 remain in the City.

Although much attention has rightly been given to the changes in the City Centre, similar, less publicised losses have taken place in what were villages but are now the suburbs where most Coventrians live. The impact of these changes is equally important to people who take a pride in the history and character of their area.

While it is not possible to bring back what has been lost, we hope this book will illustrate what is missing from modern Coventry, and will provide evidence for any future debate about what could be considered justifiable development or thoughtless destruction.

# INTRODUCTION TO THE SECOND EDITION

It has been twenty years since we finished compiling the first edition of this book and inevitably during that time there have been many more changes to the landscape of Coventry, especially in the city centre. Not all of the changes have been negative. The Phoenix Project that has given back some of the old Coventry through preservation of archaeology and conservation of threatened buildings around the old Bluecoat School and opening up new views onto the past. Also the controversial canopy associated with the Cathedral Lanes building that we featured on our first cover, has just been taken down. It was interesting to note how despite being welcomed in the Press, in the letters page, there were those who regretted its passing! It only goes to show how change in the landscape often acts as an emotional trigger that planners can rarely avoid. This is especially the case with the loss of the Hippodrome, one of the downsides to the Phoenix Project. This was a place that was associated with so many good memories of Coventry people since the late 1930s and its demolition touched the hearts of many older Coventrians.

There have been many more changes in the city centre. Apart from the Phoenix Project there is the redevelopment of the Lower Precinct and Pool Meadow. The Herbert Art Gallery and Museum refurbishment and extension together with the creation of a number of new city squares all have brought about important changes to twenty-first century Coventry. However, all of this pales into insignificance in the face of the plans for the one billion pound Jerde plan for the redevelopment of the whole Precinct over the next couple of decades. Fine words have been written about the preservation of some of the building that make up Gibson's post war vision, and wanting the plan to 'echo Coventry's medieval heritage' but time will tell how competently they have matched these aims. There are some optimistic signs that various authorities are beginning to see the value of Coventry's past at the same time as making it a city fit for the future. The preservation of the Swift car factory in Coventry University's Science Park as well as the use of the old Hotchkiss Factory as the university's Business School. The university has also preserved the old Odeon as its Performance Arts Centre. The redevelopment of Far Gosford Street by the City Council is breathing new life into the area as well as resorting an interesting set of building that have accumulated over the life of this rare medieval suburb.

With this, our first book, having been out of print for a number of years now (despite two previous reprints) we thought it we should produce a revised edition before producing a new book. This edition revises the text in the light of the changes and revelations of the last twenty years. Perhaps more importantly some of the errors from the first edition have been corrected. It is a salutatory experience to realize how with, what we thought at the time was scrupulous checking, so many mistakes were committed to print. We have also thoroughly revised and extended the section on the photographers and organisations that produced the original postcards, in the light of most recent research. To save those frustrating searches we have included an index for the first time. Finally we hope that you will find the quality of the photographs better than before thanks to improved printing technology.

# BOUNDARY EXTENSION MAP

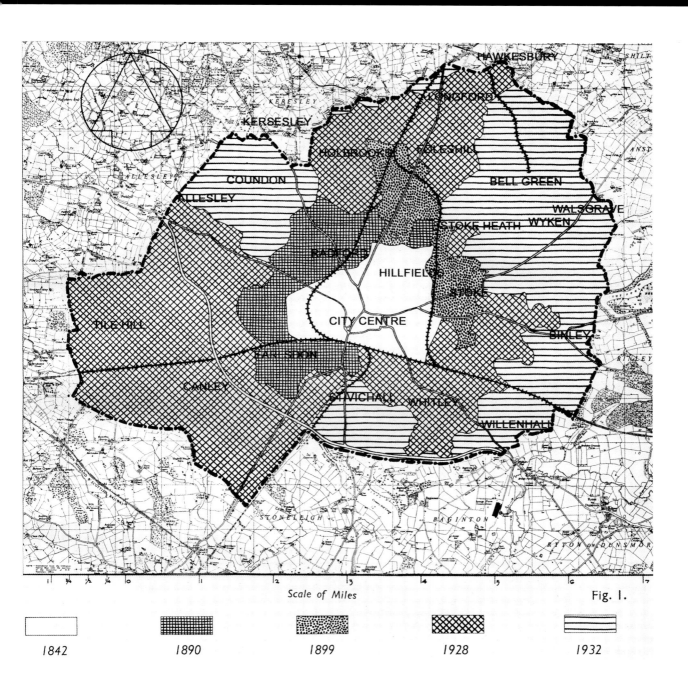

Scale of Miles

Fig. I.

| 1842 | 1890 | 1899 | 1928 | 1932 |

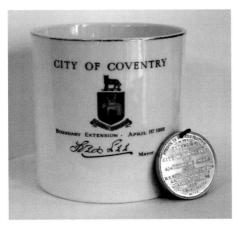

This map indicates the years when boundary extensions occurred and the villages within the extensions.

As the largest change occurred in 1928 when the city grew from 4,147 to 12,878 acres, a boundary mug and medal were issues to commemorate the occasion.

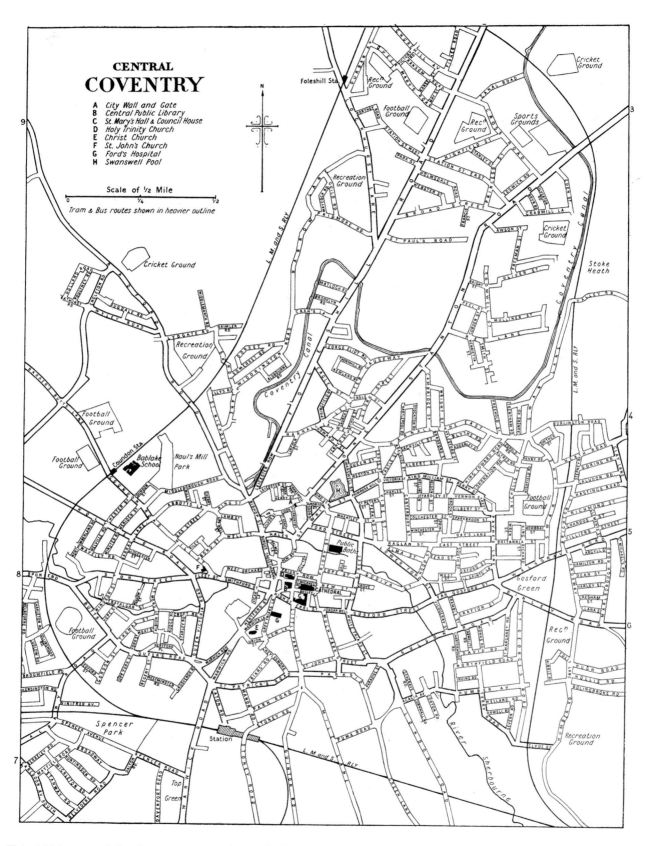

This 1931 map of the Coventry central area indicates quite clearly the main routes radiating from the heart of Coventry (i.e. Broadgate). These routes, pictorially displayed in this book, were the main arteries which were severed by the ring road.

However much the areas around Coventry can be changed with barely a word of comment, the same could never be said about the city centre itself. There is barely a building, road or open space contained within the ring road that does not evoke cries of support if there is even a hint that it might be affected by redevelopment. This is perhaps understandable considering how much change has been inflicted on this area in the last sixty years or so. Post-war changes continue to raise comment not least of which are those most recent ones to Broadgate, which if no longer quite the commercial heart of Coventry, remains its spiritual heart in the view of many Coventrians. These post-war changes alone are sufficiently vast to require a separate book to do justice to their full range. Therefore, the coverage of the city centre here will concentrate on the pre-war period. A few facts need to be borne in mind when evaluating what features have been lost from the centre (and where blame, if any, needs to be allocated). Coventry entered the Industrial Revolution very late and expanded faster than almost any other city through the early part of the twentieth century. Large parts of the medieval city had been demolished to create new roads before the Second World War and a plan for the wholesale redevelopment of the city centre had already been produced before the Blitz.

*View from the Cathedral Tower c1931 (G & Co.)*

This view, looking westwards, gives a good indication of how the city centre has completely changed, the only landmark remaining being St. John's Church seen just to the left of the Market Clock. Note also the distinctive white frontage of the recently built Burtons shop on the left. Soon the area beyond West Orchard to the right of the clock would be cleared for the building of Corporation Street. Even though the Blitz destroyed a good proportion of this part of the city centre centre, what remained was later to be demolished in line with pre-war plans. Even some significant buildings that survived, like the Gulson Library, (right foreground) and the Rudge Whitworth factory, later the G.E.C., dominating the skyline to the left were demolished in the 1980s.

7

Broadgate, is thought to take its name from the entrance to the twelfth century Coventry Castle, which stood nearby, at the intersection of two ancient trackways. These ran north, south, east and west in a similar way to how Cross Cheaping, Hertford Street, High Street and Smithford Street left Broadgate before the Second World War. As all of these routes have now been blocked by the Ring Road, we can look at them once again through the eyes of pre-war photographers.

*Broadgate c1931 (Teesee)*

The top picture is taken from in front of the Kings Head Hotel looking across to Salmon & Glucksteine's tobacconists shop on the corner of the High Street. To the right is Atkins & Turton's grocers with the very narrow Pepper Lane between it and Harrison's opticians. Down into Broadgate just to the right of the policeman can be seen Lyons Cafe. In the lower picture looking up Broadgate towards the High Street, Salmon & Glucksteine's building is again visible on the extreme right at the entrance into High Street. Although the Astley's lorry appears stationary, it is in fact entering Butcher Row, with the Royal Vaults on the corner.

*Broadgate c1926 (G & Co)*

*Broadgate c1928 (Teesee)*

This view looking down Broadgate towards Cross Cheaping shows the entrance into Butcher Row, to the right just before the Royal Vaults public house. The area cleared for the building of Trinity Street and the pre-war Owen Owen store, can be clearly appreciated from this picture. Everything on the right was demolished from just before the Whitfield's sign down to where the buildings disappear behind those on the left of Broadgate. The entry into Market Place is just opposite the Royal Vaults on the left, Boots the chemist, being on the corner. Cross Cheaping then begins.

*Market Hall & Market Street c1925
(Ana series)*

This view of the Market Hall taken from Market Street is dominated by the 100ft high tower of the Market Clock, built in 1868. The clock movement, which was made by the famous Horologist E. T. Loseby was renowned for its timekeeping. Although the Market Hall was completely destroyed in the Blitz, the clock tower was not obviously damaged. However, it was left to deteriorate until the central redevelopment commenced, when it was demolished. Clearly its position made it impossible for it to be blended into the new plan. At least the clock movement and bell were saved, being incorporated into the Godiva Clock in Broadgate.

*Cross Cheaping c1914 (Mills)*

Cross Cheaping stretched from Broadgate to the Burges, from Market Place on one side, and Butcher Row on the other. This view taken from about half way down looking towards the Burges shows David Burdett's printing and stationery shop on the right. Just below, after Lipton's grocers, was the narrow entrance to Little Butcher Row. Further down at the Broad Vaults public house was the entrance into Ironmonger Row, this being just to the right of the tram. All of this side of Cross Cheaping was demolished in 1935.

*The Burges c1939 (Unknown)*

This postcard shows the Burges, still easily recognisable today, with the clock on the right then over Gilbert's the jeweller. Just rising above it is the roof of the Old Grammar School on the corner of Hales Street. Beyond this looking up Bishop Street, nothing of this view exists today. Behind the tram is the Wine Lodge which like the rest of the buildings remains mainly unaltered. The notice on the tram indicates that it is en route to Bedworth via Bishop Street and Foleshill Road.

*The Burges c1937 (Teesee)*

This view looking into the Burges from Bishop Street shows the Wine Lodge, later the Tally Ho, now the Tudor Rose on the corner of newly opened Corporation Street, with a large sign on the wall of Glenn's, on the corner of Hales Street, advising that they sell Old Joe's Toffee. The policeman on point duty would not have been necessary before the opening of Corporation Street in 1931. The items in the sky are not birds but metal shoes on the overhead wires, to prevent the tram contact arm coming off the wires when the tram lines changed direction.

*Bishop Street c1913 (Waterman)*

This view shows Bishop Street, from the intersection with King Street which is to the right, with Leicester Street to the left. Canal House is behind the cameraman at the start of St Nicholas Street. On the corner of King Street behind the policeman is the Castle Hotel, with the Cranes Inn on the corner of Leicester Street, to the left. This intersection had to be controlled by a policeman, as traffic, especially trams, had to be given preference due to the steepness of the street. If stopped they could often not restart. The tramlines shown took trams to Bedworth via Foleshill Road.

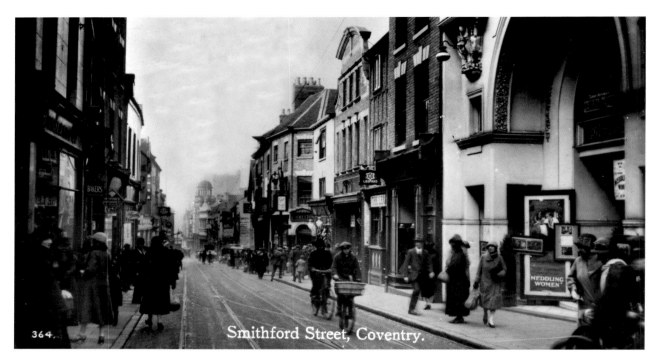

*Smithford Street c1925 (Teesee)*

This street has always been a very important route out of the city from Broadgate as any traveller to the west would pass this way. The top view, looking from Broadgate, has St John's Church in the background to the right showing over the top of the pre-war Co-op building. Immediately on the right is the Picture House, with Lionel Barrymore appearing in Meddling Woman, made in 1924 while further down past the Leopard Inn is the entrance to Market Street, with Welton's chemist on the corner. Further down still on the right past the Empire Vaults is the entrance to the Drinkwater Arcade. The bottom view looking up the street towards Broadgate being an earlier picture, shows The Great Boot Hall on the corner of West Orchard to the left, this building later being demolished to make way for the pre-war Co-op store. On the opposite side of the street on the right is the Old Baths Hotel.

*Smithford Street c1908 (Unknown)*

*Fleet Street c1908 (Unknown)*

This view is looking from Spon Street into Fleet Street showing Smithford Street further in the background with Bakers Temperance Hotel & Coffee Tavern on the right. On the opposite side of the street behind the railings is St John's Church. These railings together with the buildings behind were demolished when Corporation Street was built. Over these buildings can be seen the Market Clock Tower and the spire of Holy Trinity Church together but also the spire of St Michael's to the right.

*Spon Street c1909 (Harvey Barton)*

This view shows Spon Street leading into Fleet Street with St John's Church in the background to the left, over Soobroy's bakers on the corner of Holyhead Road. The black and white building on the left is the Rising Sun. The first part of this building is a small shop occupied by (as it states on the notice board above) E. T. Waterman, stationer who was also a postcard photographer, whose work features frequently in this book. The tram approaching is en route for Spon End and Chapelfields.

*Chapel of St James and St Christopher, Spon Street  c1932 (Unknown)*

In 1937 the City Council approved a scheme to restore the Chapel which was to include the layout of the adjoining land as a public garden At the time it was stated that it had always been the Corporations' desire to preserve the chapel, one of the city's historic showpieces. Even though Lord Kenilworth made a gift to the city which included £1,250 to purchase the Chapel and a substantial balance for the remainder of the scheme, the chapel was left to deteriorate. With additional bomb damage it was mainly demolished in 1952 but retaining its original 13th century sandstone foundations. However, it is open to the elements and gradually decaying without the protection of a roof

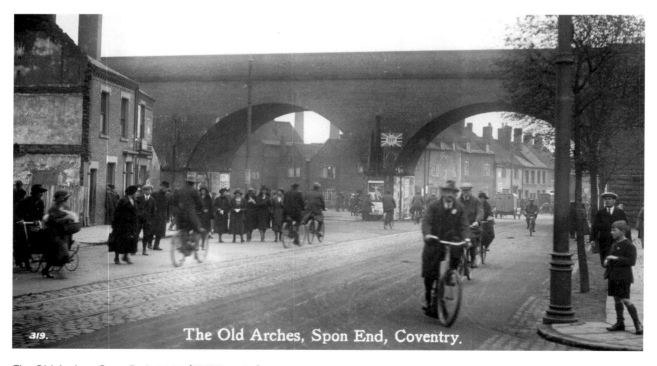

*The Old Arches, Spon End c1924 (HHT Premier)*

This picture was taken from the corner of Melbourne Road towards the Spon End railway arches. It is interesting in that it shows buildings demolished between the Black Horse Inn and the arches, where the Plaza Cinema would later be built in 1929. By the number of young ladies crossing the road it would appear that the Coventry Chain has just finished for the day. In 1857 shortly after the Coventry to Nuneaton railway line was opened, 23 of the newly built railway arches collapsed and had to be rebuilt.

*Allesley Old Road c1906 (ER)*

The top picture looking from Spon End into Chapelfields, shows Hearsall Lane to the left with Allesley Old Road stretching away in front. The importance of Chapelfields as a watchmaking area is obvious in that although there are only houses on one side of the road, trams travel all the way from Broadgate to the terminus at the corner of Mount Street. The other two streets seen on the left are Craven Street and then Duke Street. The children seen in the picture, gathered for the photograph would have attended Spon Street School as it was not until 1913 that a nearer school would be built at Centaur Road. In the lower picture taken further along Allesley Old Road, it can be seen how relatively narrow the main road to Allesley is compared to today. Passengers who took the tram from Broadgate to the terminus at Chapelfields but lived in Allesley would have to walk the rest of the way along this route.

*Allesley Old Road c1910 (Waterman)*

*High Street Corner c1926 (Teesee)*

This busy street scene looking from Broadgate into the High Street shows the Coventry Arms and the old National Provincial Bank, before they were demolished in 1929 to make way for the new bank of the same name. The other buildings just the other side of Greyfriars Lane were also demolished to make way for the new Lloyds Bank. The policeman with the white helmet seems to be struggling to bring the traffic under control. Salmon & Glucksteine who were the most prominent tobacconists in the city can be seen on the corner of Broadgate. The fully cobbled road would not survive the war.

*The Cathedral from Pepper Lane c1932 (Teesee)*

This view is looking towards the Cathedral from the end of Pepper Lane where it meets Bayley Lane. It shows Derby Lane to the left with Frank Downey, tailor on the corrner. Further up Bayley Lane on the left can be seen County Hall with the Golden Cross opposite on the corner of Hay Lane. In the foreground on the right, at the end of Pepper Lane is the Toby's Head.

*High Street c1912 (A&G Taylor)*

This view, looking from High Street towards Broadgate, shows on the left the Craven Arms Hotel an early coaching inn which was rebuilt soon after this picture was taken . Further down on the same side Waters & Co, wine and spirit merchants, founded in 1802 have their premises. On the opposite side on the far corner of Pepper Lane, Atkins & Turton Ltd grocers, are in a fine building, which in later years was to become Martins Bank. This building has more recently been demolished for the construction of Cathedral Lanes, and the Craven Arms has also been replaced by a new Bank building. Waters have now moved to a new location away from the city. This important street has now lost much of its character as a shopping area.

*The Council House, Earl Street  c1923 (HHT Premier)*

This picture is of Earl Street looking towards Jordan Well showing a very recognisable Council House on the left, but nothing to the right exists today. Earl Street was once a busy area with shops on both sides of the street, but just before the building of the Council House began in 1913 the shops on that side were demolished. When the Council House was officially opened in 1920 by HRH the Duke of York, later to become King George VI, this view remained the same until the Blitz. Gibberd & Son, clothiers can be seen on the far corner of Little Park Street, on the right. After the war modern Council House extensions were built on the opposite side of Earl Street and a bridge was erected to join the buildings which has diminished the appearance of the original frontage.

*The Cathedral c1929 (Teesee)*

The old Cathedral Church of St Michael was mainly built in the 14th century and completed in 1433 when the 300ft spire was added. In 1918 the Bishopric and Diocese of Coventry was constituted and the church was raised to the status of a Cathedral. In the top view, the outside is seen from the east, the car in the foreground travelling up Priory Street. The lower picture showing the interior, is a view taken from the Nave looking towards the High Altar. The Cathedral was destroyed in the Blitz on the night of 14th November 1940, only the shell together with the tower and spire remained. When the new Cathedral was built, part of the north facing wall of the old Cathedral was demolished to enable the two buildings to be linked. The new Cathedral was consecrated in 1962.

*Interior, Coventry Cathedral c1929 (Teesee)*

*Old Palace Yard, Earl Street c1910 (Kingsway)*

This most interesting quadrangle stood in Earl Street, almost opposite where the Council House would be built a few years after this picture was taken. It was one of the most striking examples of domestic architecture in the city, with styles ranging from the 15th to 17th century. Unfortunately despite its restoration in the inter-war years, most of the buildings were destroyed in the Blitz and those that remained were demolished to make way for the Council House extensions.

*Cox Street c1911 (Waterman)*

A short detour from our route, into Cox Street is required to show this wonderful view which is just below Cope Street. The children are outside B. Haymes, stationer and newsagent, who in addition to selling the Daily Sportsman and Racing World, also has a large selection of picture postcards in his window. The Walsall Arms is just behind with Evans & Co pawnbrokers further down. On the opposite side the entrance into Godiva Street can be seen, and further down on the same side is the taller building of the Stevengraph Works of Thomas Stevens which is next to the Sydenham Palace on the corner of Lower Ford Street.

*Hotchkiss Factory, Gosford Street c1916 (Sylvester)*

This interesting postcard dated 29th January 1916, shows the Hotchkiss Factory being built in Gosford Street. Erected to produce guns and other munitions during the First World War, it turned to producing car engines when the war ended. It was acquired by William Morris (later Lord Nuffield) in 1926 then becoming Morris Motors Ltd, Engines Branch. Since the Second World War, when it again produced munitions, it had been used by the Department of Social Security. But unlike the similar pioneering steel framed Rudge factory in Spon Street, this building was saved from demolition by Coventry University. Like the nearby Odeon that they also purchased it has been carefully preserved and converted for academic use. The horse & cart are outside the premises of F. Collins, furniture dealer, later to be demolished.

*Gosford Street c1912 (Waterman)*

With little to fear for life or limb, the photographer has set his tripod in the middle of "busy" Gosford Street, looking up towards town. In fact where he is standing was the site of Gosford Gate, one of the main entrances through the ancient city wall. Gosford Street was well endowed with pubs then, and of the five in this view, only one survives - the Peacock, and even that is a later building. The five pubs were, on the left the Antelope and the Peacock whilst on the right were the New Inn (just beyond the shop blinds), the Fox and Vivian and the Old Chase. Just beside the New Inn was an entrance to one of the courts that contained The Alfa Motor Works, a less successful motor manufacturer which failed with many others in the late 1920's.

*All Saint's Church, Far Gosford Street c1925 (HHT Premier)*

This church, built in Far Gosford Street and consecrated in 1869 is typical of many churches of this period that were built in the early English style with local red sandstone. It was demolished in 1970, it would appear without reason, because nothing was built in it's place. Often small churches like this and St Thomas's in the Butts, also demolished in 1975, have outgrown the needs of reduced congregations. But their loss often means that the visual relief that they and their churchyards give in otherwise built-up areas is lost. In this instance this is not true as the wall and avenue of trees remain.

*Far Gosford Street c1926 (G & Co)*

This postcard shows the Hertford Arms on the right next to the Scala Picture House. The building jutting out closer to the pavement is Cook's, draper's which at the time was an agent for Twilfit British-made corsets. On the left on the corner of Court 10, is Rayner's Fried Fish Saloon with the car parked outside the City Bargain Stores, who were drapers. The tram further up the street will at Gosford Green turn right along Binley Road to the terminus just past the  Bulls Head' public house. The plan of restorations and improvements in this street area is a rare story of reviving an area of the city through focusing on its inherited streetscape.

*The Humber Motor Works, Far Gosford Street c1906 (E.R.)*

This building, soon to be hidden at ground level by an assortment of shops (as can be seen below), was one of a number fated to be owned by the Humber Company and suffer subsequent damage by fire! Their first Coventry premises in Lower Ford Street were burnt down in 1896/7 and the business was scattered about the Midlands. One part became established in this building, the old factory of Townsend Bros., Cycle Manufacturers. However, true to form, in December 1906, a few weeks after this photograph was taken, the premises were severely damaged. This hastened the move to a new factory already planned in Folly Lane (later called Humber Road).

*Far Gosford Street c1912 (Waterman later republished by H.H.T. Premier)*

This view is not so different from that seen today, yet three short years before this photograph was taken, it would have looked quite different. There would have been almost no shops to be seen and the large building on the corner would have easily been recognised as the recently vacated Humber Motor Works (see above). Beside the Humber was a pretty terrace of mid-Victorian cottages. By 1912, however, almost all properties had been converted into retail businesses of one kind or another, e.g. grocer, ironmonger, baker, fruiterer, butcher, draper, tailor, fishmonger, etc. as they are still today. Some of the integrity of the Humber building has returned with its partial conversion by Lloyds Bank.

*King's Head Hotel, Hertford Street c1926 (Teesee)*

Hertford Street, which owes it's name to the Marquess of Hertford who originally owned the land on which it was built, was not constructed until 1812. Until then the route from Broadgate to Kenilworth and Warwick, was via Greyfriars Lane, Warwick Lane and Warwick Row. It was the major tram route from the railway station to Broadgate. The top view looking from Broadgate towards Greyfriars Green, shows the King's Head, Coventry's premier hotel, later destroyed in the 1940 Blitz. Beyond this, however, the Empire Theatre - which later became a cinema - and many other buildings on either side of the street, although damaged, were repaired and remained until the street was finally closed to traffic in 1969. The bottom view looking towards Broadgate shows the Kenilworth Castle public house on the extreme left with the Geisha Cafe next door, which was a favourite meeting place for shoppers and theatre goers. The last reminder of these early days was the sign 'Luckmans Pianos' painted on the side of the roof of one of the buildings on the right hand side. It has recently been painted over.

*Hertford Street c1913 (Mills)*

*Hertford Street c1910 (WY)*

These two views show all three of the Coventry Spires, taken from almost the same spot. The top view looking up Hertford Street shows Holy Trinity with St. Michael's seen to the right over buildings in Warwick Lane. On the extreme left is the Three Tuns Hotel, with the Peeping Tom public house just beyond, on the other side of Bull Yard. The Three Tuns was an early coaching inn, built before 1750. It was resited in 1965, the original building being demolished soon afterwards. The building on the right, on the corner of Union Street, is also seen in the lower picture, being the premises of J. W. Lazenby, Railway and Shipping Agent. On the other side of Union Street, to the right was the Liberal Club which was demolished when the street was widened and it became New Union Street. In the centre is Christ Church, built in 1830 but incorporating the 14th century tower and spire of the former Greyfriars Church. Christ Church was bombed in 1940, the body of the Church being reduced to a shell. The ruins were eventually demolished, only the tower and spire now remaining.

*Christ Church, Union Street c1924 (Dania)*

*The Manor House, Cheylesmore c1926 (Teesee)*

A short detour along Union Street, past the intersection of Cow Lane and Greyfriars Lane into Cheylesmore would have brought you to the gatehouse of Cheylesmore Manor. The 13th century manor lay between the gatehouse and what is now Friars Road. All that remained of the manor house after the war was most of the south wing with its magnificent timbered roof. But in 1955 it was demolished. The gatehouse remained and fortunately was saved and restored in 1967 becoming the Coventry Registry Office.

*Swift Car Factory, Mile Lane c1910 (WY)*

At the end of Cheylesmore at the intersection with St Patrick's Road once stood Cheylesmore Gate, which before the city wall and gates were demolished would have taken travellers into Cheylesmore Park. The cameraman who took this picture would have stood on the site of the gate. The view shows the Swift Motor & Cycle Works, in Quinton Road, the radiator company on the left, being on the corner of Parkside. The Swift Works which originally included Edward's House on the corner of Mile Lane, seen on the extreme right. At the time of the first edition of this book it was under threat of demolition, but the subsequent outcry led to its conversion into a hotel with the façade preserved.

*Warwick Road, showing Three Spires c1928 (Teesee)*

This view shows Warwick Road with Queen's Road to the left, and Greyfriars Green just beyond, behind ornamental railings. St Patrick's Road and Eaton Road are behind the Policeman to the right. The large houses seen behind the trees are 'Darlaston' on the corner, then 'Park Gate' and 'Park House', all of which were demolished to build a slip road on to the Ring Road. Further down, past the YMCA, is the Quadrant, over which can be seen the three spires.

*Eaton Road c1925 (Ana series)*

This view shows Eaton Road leading to the railway station with Park Road behind the parked car on the left. The tram at the station terminus will leave for Broadgate. The station was built in phases between 1846 and 1904. It was badly damaged in the 1940 Blitz but continued to operate until the new station opened in 1962. Although Eaton Road still exists, the greater part of this view would is taken up with Station Square.

The Three Spires, Coventry.

*Warwick Road c1925 (Teesee)*

Both of these views show Warwick Road, the top one where the road is intersected by Queen's Road to the left and St Patrick's Road and Eaton Road on the right. The policeman who controlled this busy junction can be seen in the middle of the road. In addition to the various forms of transport seen, trams also travelled to and from the Railway Station to Broadgate, the route being, Eaton Road, Warwick Road and Hertford Street. The buildings on the left, known as Lansdowne Place, included nearest the camera, Perkins & Sons, nurserymen, next to the entrance to the railway goods depot. These buildings were demolished when the Ring Road was constructed and Park Court (now also demolished!) was built on this site. The lower view, looking towards the city centre from the Kenilworth road end shows, to the left, Top Green behind ornamental railings with, on the right, large private houses. One of these, The Hylands, is now a hotel.

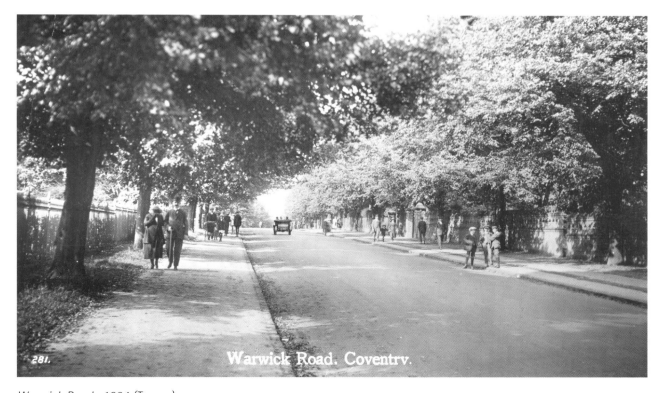

Warwick Road. Coventry.

*Warwick Road c1924 (Teesee)*

*Opera House, Hales Street c1910*
*(Harvey Barton)*

The Opera House was built in 1889 in Hales Street, next to the Old Grammar School. It became the home of the Coventry Repertory Company in 1931. After it was badly damaged in 1940, it was repaired and converted into a cinema. Finally it was demolished in 1961, the modern buildings which have taken its place show little respect for the neighbouring Old Grammar School, which is one of Coventry's oldest buildings.

*New Hippodrome, Hales Street c1938 (Valentines)*

This view along Hales Street towards Corporation Street, shows the New Hippodrome soon after it was opened in November 1937. The architect Stanley Hattrell was the son of the architect of the Old Hippodrome built in 1906. The new building seated 2,000 people. With interior decoration carried out by the company who did similar work on the liner "Queen Mary", the Hippodrome set new standards of comfort for the audience. The art deco exterior can be compared with the Victorian Opera House, seen further along Hales Street. The fate of this building has become clearer since the first edition of this book as it was demolished to make way for Millennium Place.

*The Hippodrome, Hales Street c1910 (Harvey Barton)*

The first Hippodrome was a corrugated iron structure on Pool Meadow. In 1904 it was decided that a more permanent building was needed so it was constructed and opened next to Swanswell Gate on December 21st 1906. At the time of this photograph Harry Lauder was appearing. The building was demolished in 1938 soon after the New Hippodrome was opened alongside it. Lady Herbert's Garden now takes up some of this site.

*Swanswell Gate , Hales Street c1915 (EB)*

Seen in this picture with part of the Old Hippodrome on the left, Swanswell Gate with Cook Street, are all that now remain of the original twelve city gates. It is shown with a roof and chimney which were later removed. The upper part of the gate still housed several families, the ground level being used as a fruit-shop. The large notice on the side of the gate advertises John Astley & Sons, tent, sheet and rope makers, with offices in Broadgate. The smaller notices below advertise sales of property and livestock including 35 horses.

*The Fire Station, Hales Street c1913 (A Mills later published by T H Co)*

The Fire Station was built in 1902 in Hales Street opposite to where the Old Hippodrome was built later. Seen to the left are two cottages where the station officer together with his assistant and their families lived. Some years after this picture, these cottages were demolished, the station being extended to add three further bays which is much the same as it is today. Next to the cottages is seen the entrance into Pool Meadow, then Trinity Schools on the corner of Ford Street. The Fire Station is no longer under threat of demolition having been converted into an eating and entertainment venue.

*Art Schools, Ford Street c1908 (Kingsway)*

In 1858 a proposal was made for a School of Art and Design to be built to give instruction on design relative to the ribbon and watch trades in the city. In 1863 the building seen here was opened and served the city, until it was damaged by bombing in October 1940. After the war the building was repaired and some classes moved back from the overcrowded annex at Hillcrest, Radford Road. Unfortunately the building, unused after 1959, was demolished together with Trinity Schools, seen to the right, to make way for the inner ring road.

*White Street c1925 (Teesee)*

This view looking along White Street towards the Swanswell, shows Ford Street on the right, with just past the lamp post Lawrence Bros, ironmongers. The shops beyond include Batts outfitters and Hawkesford's confectioner. On the far corner of Jesson Street to the left is Goddard & Poke, wholesale newsagents with further along on the corner of Norton Street the Sir Thomas White Hotel. The tram lines running up Jesson Street are for trams to Bell Green, with trams for Hillfields and Stoke passing up White Street.

*The Swanswell, White Street c1928 (Teesee)*

This view shows Swanswell Pool, when it was used for boating as well as fishing. The boats which had small cranked handles to each paddle wheel enabled young boys to manoeuvre and explore what was known as 'Treasure Island' in the middle of the pool. White Street can be seen and over the shops part of the roof of Robbins & Powers flour mill, later Goodwins, in Wheatley Street.

*View from Old Hippodrome roof c1936 (Unknown)*

The top view is not a scene of destruction after the Blitz, but an earlier scene of destruction, when much of the medieval heart of Coventry, covering about three acres, was levelled to make way for Trinity Street and the pre-war Owen Owen store. The view is looking towards Broadgate, with the Fire Station and New Buildings to the left. The buildings directly in front, were also shortly to be demolished to make way for the New Hippodrome which was opened in 1937. The bottom view looking from Broadgate, down the Burges and Trinity Street, has the newly opened Owen Owen store in the foreground. This store was only to last two years before it too was destroyed in the Blitz. It is interesting to compare this view with that shown at the top of page 9, to realise just how much was demolished. The legacy of this store is still with us as its extensive cellars held up building work on the city council project to create Ironmonger Square on this site.

*Burges & Trinity Street c1938 (Valentines)*

*Pilgrims Rest, Palmer Lane c1910*
*(Harvey Barton)*

This inn and lodging house, on the corner of Palmer Lane and Ironmonger Row, is typical of many interesting buildings demolished in the mid-thirties to enable Trinity Street to be built. As can be seen on the notice above the door, the Pilgrims Rest was built in 1820 on the site of the guest-house of the Monastery which once stood on a spot near Priory Row. Pilgrims who came to worship at the nearby St Mary's Benedictine monastery were able to take shelter at the guest house.

*Butcher Row c1908 (Unknown)*

This charming scene showing a lady in Edwardian dress buying fruit, hardly compares with the view today from the same spot looking down Trinity Street. This view down Butcher Row towards Little Butcher Row and the Bull Ring, shows clearly the medieval buildings of various types which were destroyed in the creation of Trinity Street. If a point of reference is required, Priory Row is to the right just past Palmers, furniture dealer's sign. Behind the cameraman to his left, is the entrance from Broadgate.

*Cook Street Gate c1910 (EB)*

This view shows Cook Street when still part of the main thoroughfare from Bishop Street to Stoney Stanton Road. At this time Cook Street Gate is just a shell. It was saved from further decay in 1913 when it was purchased by Sir William Wyley and presented to the City. It was then renovated and part of its roof and windows reconstructed (seen in the view below). The Ye Old Tower Inn, seen attached to the gate, closed in 1915 and converted into a pair of cottages.

*Cook Street Gate from Lady Herbert's Garden c1939 (Valentines)*

Although the building of Lady Herbert's Garden began in 1930, it was not until the Old Hippodrome was demolished in 1938, following the opening of the New Hippodrome that the work could be completed. The area from the City Wall to Chauntry Place was then cleared to enable the Gardens to be laid out together with cottages for twelve elderly ladies to be constructed. The full cost of the work was covered by a gift to the city by Sir Alfred Herbert, in memory of his wife. At the time of the picture, it can be seen that Cook Street Gate has been repaired and new battlements added. At this time the old cottages are still attached to the side, but in 1963 they were demolished, the new commercial building that took their place overpowering the gate. Various features from the Phoenix Project have also changed the views around the garden making it feel less peaceful.

*Public Baths, Priory Street c1910 (Kingsway)*

When these Public Baths were opened in 1894 in Priory Street, opposite Pool Meadow, it not only offered first class swimming facilities, but with an Assembly Room, could also cater for large public functions. As it was built in what was then largely a residential area, like the Slipper Baths in Hillfields, it could also provide private washing facilities for people whose homes did not have bathrooms. Although effected by bomb damage, it did carry on into the 1950s until demolished. The site is now part of Pool Meadow car park.

*The Sydenham Palace, Cox Street c1910 (Harvey Barton)*

The Sydenham Palace was built on the corner of Lower Ford Street and Cox Street in 1867 In its heyday it was comparable to the Kings Head and the Craven Arms as a place of entertainment. It was not only a public house but a music hall, being granted a full music license in 1891. At that time it was advertised as a Theatre of Varieties with first class artistes changed weekly. Being a building with architectural merit and with its historic cultural background, it was a great pity that not long after it closed in 1971 it was demolished.

*St Thomas's Church, Albany Road c1910 (Kingsway)*

When built in 1848, St Thomas's Church would have been in open fields on the edge of the City. But later the area was built up and it stood at the corner of the Butts and Albany Road. It was consecrated in 1849 to serve the parish of St Thomas, this parish being created out of St John the Baptist. The stone for the church was given by Lord Leigh of Stoneleigh Abbey and came from a quarry on his Estate near the Kenilworth Road. Despite being a notable example of Gothic revival architecture, the church was demolished and the site redeveloped in 1975.

*Gulson Library, Trinity Lane c1910 (Kingsway)*

The Public Free Library was also known as Gulson Library as John Gulson, a Coventry mayor, paid for the library to be built. It was opened in 1873 and later extended in 1890. It was situated on the corner of Derby Lane and Trinity Lane, opposite Holy Trinity Church. It was partly destroyed in 1940 but what remained continued to be used as a lending library before being demolished to make way for the Cathedral Lanes development.

# ALLESLEY

Allesley which was, until taken into the City in 1928, administered by Meriden Rural District Council, has retained much of its character and charm. This is surprising for the village was under far more threat than other villages on the outskirts of Coventry, due the volume of traffic which passed through the village before the by-pass was opened in 1966. The fact that Allesley is now the only traditional village centre remaining in Coventry, is mainly due to the local residents and conservationists whose efforts resulted in the village being designated a Conservation area in December 1968.

At the time of the first edition of this book Allesley residents had just lost the battle to stop the Jaguar relief road across the Coundon Wedge. If only they had known then what the future of Jaguar was to be then some valuable green belt land would not have been lost. As it is the road simply excuses further development in this attractive area.

*Birmingham Road c1904 (Unknown)*

In 1904 when this postcard was sent the Rainbow Inn, built in 1680, would have been one of many pubs on the busy coaching road to Holyhead. This inn would have been at the centre of the social life of the community and a meeting place for sportsmen, evident by the poster that the publican and horse dealer Samuel Anthoney has in the doorway, advertising a Rudge Whitworth Cycle Race Meeting in Coventry. The original steepness of the road up into the village from Coventry was considerably reduced in height when the Holyhead Road was built in the early nineteenth century. This can be seen by the banks remaining on either side of the road, and the steps up to the cottages and front door of the Rainbow.

*Birmingham Road c1910 (Blakeman & Saville)*

This postcard shows a group of children outside the Victorian school which is just out of the picture to the right. This school, opened in 1874, served the village until the present primary school was opened early in the 1960's in Antrim Close. It would seem that the children may have gathered to see the car, fast disappearing into the distance towards the church, as this would have been quite a novelty at that time.

*Allesley Church and Rectory, Rectory Lane c1932 (Teesee)*

All Saints Church was originally built about 1130 then substantially rebuilt in 1863 but is little altered today. The Old Rectory however, originally built in 1779 and enlarged in 1863, was demolished in 1962 and replaced by a new Rectory which is quite out of character with the Church. What a great pity that an alternative use could not have been found for the Old Rectory. It would have been a fitting memorial to the Rev. Bree, who had it built, and who, with the other five Bree Rectors, gave over 150 years of continuous service to the church and the community between 1749 and 1917.

*Birmingham Road & Old Toll Gate c1932 (Teesee)*

This view taken looking towards the Toll Gate, shows what was to become Paybody Hospital on the left. This building originally known as "The Elms" had been a private house for over 300 years, but at the time of the picture had just become a Convalescent Home, being presented in 1929 to the Coventry Crippled Children's Guild by Thomas Paybody. After being improved in 1938, first becoming an Orthopaedic Hospital and then an Eye Hospital, it has now closed and opened as pub and restaurant, taking on the old name of the house.

*Toll Gate House, Allesley Old Road c1925 (Teesee)*

This toll house stood at the intersection of the Holyhead Road and Allesley Old Road and originally had gates across both roads. A toll was charged to users of the Holyhead or Turnpike Road to defray the cost of building the Thomas Telford Road between 1828 and 1831. The Toll House was demolished during road widening in the mid 1930's, the only reminder of its existence being the Toll Gate Inn, an interesting example of art deco architecture but currently under threat of demolition.

# BINLEY

In 1900 Binley had less time than most of Coventry's satellite villages to enjoy its rural, almost feudal way of life. By 1907 a colliery was being constructed that would dominate village life until its closure in 1963. This change was more notable than in most other surrounding settlements as it ended a period of stability, under the patronage of the owners of Coombe Abbey that had lasted for 750 years. The Cravens of Coombe who had been lords of the manor for more than 300 years of that time sold up in 1922, though they had long given up using the Abbey as their principal residence in preference to their seat in Berkshire. Many farms and cottages now had owner occupiers for the first time ever, one example of a positive development brought by the twentieth century.

Today Binley is very much a part of Coventry with much development on all open land encouraged by the building of the Eastern By-pass and the development of Binley Park School playing fields since the school was closed in July 1990

*Binley Bridge, Binley Road c1905 (Unknown)*

This scene is very evocative of time past with these two old-timers enjoying a peaceful chat on old Binley Bridge, however, they would be in real danger if they tried doing the same thing on this spot today. The location is where the Binley Road is carried over the River Sowe, looking towards Coventry. Nowadays the bridge is wider than it is long, to accommodate the dual carriageway that approaches the traffic lights at the junction of Binley Road and Allard Way. For many years this original bridge was in great danger of being swept away by the occasional floods that swelled the River Sowe. At such times heavy traction engines were placed on the apex of the bridge for extra support. Today the water table is so much lower that the current of the Sowe is never very strong.

*Binley Colliery, Willenhall Lane c1925 (Teesee)*

Construction of the colliery began in May 1907 by the Glasgow firm of Merry & Cunningham. It was worked for the last time on Friday 15th February 1963. Although it meant a loss of jobs, at the time they were reasonably plentiful elsewhere in the city. Also the closing of the pit did bring an end to an unpleasant source of pollution. But more sadly it marked the start of the erosion of the community based about the pit. Travel and accommodation being difficult in Edwardian times meant that the developers of Binley Colliery had to build their own village on site to house the miners, many of whom came from other parts of the country. The houses varied in size according to the head of the household's status at the pit. These houses, below, fronting Willenhall Lane would have been occupied by the overseers.

*Abbey Cottages, Willenhall Lane c1925 (Teesee)*

41

*The Craven Arms, Binley c1925 (Teesee)*

The village pub as it is pictured here has only a couple of years left before it would be radically transformed into the mock Tudor look it retains today. It is worth noting that the pub sign is reputed to be the last painted by the Victorian Coventry artist David Gee, who died in 1872. Despite the air of rustic charm the nearby pit was already making its impact here as the colliery male voice choir could be heard practicing at the pub in the evenings.

*The Maypole at St Bartholomews Church, Binley c1910 (Unknown)*

There is little more to say than what the picture tells us; a communal celebration of May Day that involves much of the village. Though infrequent, holidays were a real cause for celebration at the turn of the century. It is possible that these were children from Willenhall school who were recorded as performing in Whitley, Willenhall and Binley, carrying their maypole before them.

# COUNDON

A flavour of the old Coundon can still be appreciated by a wander through that rare stretch of green in the city, Coundon Wedge, (apart from the link road built for the Jaguar factory). It is a landscape of twisting narrow lanes, small hedge fields, trees, streams, ponds and the occasional farmhouse. The original Coundon was little different. There was never a village centre as such, perhaps a small settlement near Coundon Court. However, by the last century the hamlet at Brownshill Green provided the focus of what village life there was in the area, while nearby Keresley shared any missing facilities.

The character of Coundon began to change with the arrival of wealthy house hunters from Coventry in the latter part of the 19th century. The attraction of healthy living in this area of relatively high ground, where there was not a monopoly of ownership, as in so many other of Coventry's satellite villages, meant a real growth in the construction of large houses, especially along the Tamworth Road. This was to prove only the beginning of the urban invasion and today only the foresight of those who protected the Coundon Wedge prevents a complete loss of the past.

*Barker Butts Lane, Westhill c1939 (Richards)*

This view has not changed substantially since this photograph was taken in the late 1930's. This was yet another estate built during a period of frantic pre-war building in Coventry. The change in the district was sufficiently drastic for the Midland Daily Telegraph to comment in 1936: "Try to imagine Barker Butts as a narrow country path leading from the Coundon Station level crossing on to a farm at the top of the fields to the top of the hill, whence could be obtained an uninterrupted view of the city of those days. That was possible as recently as 1925. Now it is a suburb.........wherein there are 6,000 houses occupied by a population of 20,000 in 100 new streets". Today it is just possible to see two of the three spires faintly visible in this picture, but with the trees more fully grown only the wide awake driver will spot them. The Cedars pub retains its name but has unfortunately lost some of the characteristic art deco detailing of its original architecture.

*Gardeners Cottage, "The Elms", Coundon Green c1906 (Unknown)*

This is probably the only surviving building from the original hamlet of Coundon that was based around the area near Coundon Court School. Its description on the original postcard was of the gardener's cottage at The Elms, which was the name by which Coundon Lodge was known in Edwardian times. Though in part dating from the seventeenth century the cottage is basically medieval at heart making it one of the oldest buildings this side of Coventry. Fortunately it survives, but minus its thatched roof.

*Nugget Inn, Coundon Green c1925 (Teesee)*

A few years ago the one clue to the location of this pub would have been missing as its name had been changed to the Sky Blue. Furthermore it has been rebuilt, since this postcard was published, a short distance from its original location opposite Northbrook Road. It has now reverted to its original name but remains the large suburban pub typical of so many erected this century in Coventry to cater for the increased custom from the new estates.

Earlsdon shares much of its history with Spon End and Chapelfields. It was the boom in the watchmaking trade that caused the need to expand from Spon End into Chapelfields which began in 1847 when Craven Street and the surrounding area was developed. Then in 1851, following the purchase of 30 acres of prime farm land between Hearsall and Styvechale Commons, by the Coventry Freehold Land Society, this spread continued into what is now Earlsdon. Even after the decline of the watchmaking industry, Earlsdon continued to expand, becoming one of the most favourable residential districts around Coventry.

In 1890 Earlsdon was incorporated into the City, but it was still virtually cut off from the City. It was not until 1897 when Albany Road was opened that development gained momentum. The City tramway system was soon extended along the Butts up Albany Road into the main shopping area, which quickly grew. New streets were being laid out all around the area, eventually land between Earlsdon and Chapelfields was developed, mainly by the Newcombe Brothers of Market Harborough, Newcombe Road which bears their name being completed in 1905. By 1918 the area was fully developed, much as it is today, and with little redevelopment Earlsdon has retained much of its original character and charm.

*Earlsdon Stores & Off-Licence, Providence Street, Cromwell Street c1912 (Unknown)*

The charm of early Earlsdon before the First World War is clearly illustrated in this view, which shows the Earlsdon Stores and Off-Licence. This building exists today, still operating as an off-licence, on the corner of Cromwell Street, which was later renamed Berkeley Road South. George Harris seen with his wife, daughter and dog, looks very proud of his premises, the delivery cart indicating the address as being 40 Cromwell Street. The fact that he is an agent for Mitchells & Butlers is also clearly shown.

*Albany Road c1913 (Mills)*

Albany Road was named after HRH the Duchess of Albany who came to Coventry in November 1898, brought new life into Earlsdon. The tram and other road users, together with the train passing over the bridge on the Nuneaton line, gave the photographer a scene worth recording. The high poles carrying the tram wires, the ornate streetlamps, together with the train signals showing over the roof of the Albany Hotel complete the scene.

*Albany Road c1913 (Mills)*

This view looking down Albany Road, from Earlsdon Street, shows the new library completed in 1912. This together with those at Foleshill and Stoke were built by the benefaction of the Scottish-American steel magnate Andrew Carnegie, who was made an Hon-Freeman of the City in 1914 for his generosity. Although the tram track up Albany Road was only single, the small island on which the children are standing would appear to be the point at which the trams passed each other.

*Earlsdon Avenue c1910 (Waterman)*

Earlsdon School was originally opened in November 1890 by the Coventry School Board and was enlarged in 1905, to include an upper level of classrooms. It can be seen to the right of the tree. Two years later Earlsdon Library was built. beside the school. Some remnants of the open countryside remain like the large tree, dangerously near to the road.  It was a few more years before it was cut down in 1914. The new Methodist Church was not built on the corner opposite the library until 1923. At this time the Methodist Church was in Cromwell Street, the building later became the Criterion Theatre.

*Earlsdon Centre c1916 (TT series)*

This view looking up Earlsdon Street from the Albany Road junction is interesting in that it shows a wooden fence around the City Arms'. This public house known affectionately as 'Ma Cooper's' was demolished in the late 1930s when the existing pub of the same name was built. The next building however on the same side, the Imperial Cinema, later to become the Continental, was to remain until the early 1960s, when it was demolished to make way for modern shops and offices.

*Earlsdon Street c1925 (HHT Premier)*

At first glance both of these views show little change from today. The top picture shows the Co-operative Society grocer on the corner of Poplar Road. In the next building, built in 1907, A. Keight's shoe factory is on the left with the Empire Meat Co and H. Moore baker being the other occupants. The buildings between this and the Earlsdon Working Men's Club were all demolished in the late 1980s to make way for a modern Co-op store. The lower picture looking down Earlsdon Street towards the library shows Mr Garlick, gents' hairdresser, in his white overall, standing outside his shop. The other shops beyond include, Boots Chemist, J Thomas, ironmonger and Talbot & Sons, motor and cycle depot. Although altered at ground level, most of the shop frontages down to the horse and cart, remain unchanged, however, past Providence Street, on both sides, modern bank and shops premises have been built. It seems a particular shame that in this context so many architects have failed to take account of the context in which their buildings are set.

*Earlsdon Street c1914 (G & Co)*

# FOLESHILL (including BELL GREEN and HAWKESBURY)

The area that is Foleshill has never been particularly easy to define, being more a scattering of hamlets rather than an area with a clearly defined central focus. For most Coventrians it is best understood as the neighbourhood surrounding the Foleshill and Stoney Stanton roads. Both these roads provided a lifeline of industrial development for a city centre choked by the unavailability of land for development in other directions. The existence of the Coventry Canal and Coventry to Nuneaton Railway in the same locality only served to confirm Foleshill's suitability for industry. It was an area already partly developed by the nineteenth century, let alone the 20th. Certainly industries such as Cash's ribbon weaving factory, the Ordnance Works and various brick works were already established in the area. In addition suburban development had built up along many of the roads in lower Foleshill by 1900. Twentieth century changes have not helped the development of clearly identifiable centres of community life for Foleshill; it is characterised more as a continuous flow of human activity along the two main roads. Despite the development and subsequent decline) of important factories in the Foleshill area the most noticeable changes have come in the outer reaches of Foleshill. Where in areas such as Bell Green development of communities has been more about large housing estates than truly mixed community development as found elsewhere in Foleshill.

## 365, FOLESHILL ROAD, COVENTRY.

*365 Foleshill Road c1905 (Unknown)*

This shop was to be found on the west side of the Foleshill Road at the entrance to Lockhurst Lane. At that time there was a farm where Courtaulds old factory now stands. The church is shown in the drawing is a touch of artistic licence as the nearest church was in the opposite direction! The Youngs who owned the shop only lived there for a couple more years after this drawing was made, but the shop lived on until it too was demolished in a later Courtauld expansion.

*J & J Cash Ltd., Cash's Lane c1910 (Waterman)*

It would be impossible to reproduce the above view of the factory today due to the erection of industrial buildings surrounding this silk ribbon weaving factory. The Cash brothers built their factory in 1857 just outside the town in what was officially rural Radford. The proximity of the canal was, by then, largely irrelevant to the needs of this type of manufacture. With the workers living on the bottom two floors, and the factory located on the top floor, it was an unusual development in the history of the Industrial Revolution. Therefore it is pleasing to note its present state of preservation. The busy view (below) of Cash's Lane with the factory in the background, illustrates the importance of this route at the time, as the first crossing point of the canal since leaving the basin in Drapers Field, though the poor state of the road would not seem to support its status. Note the canal bridge was very narrow at this time causing a traffic hold up at busy times so was widened at a cost of £700 in 1912.

*Cash's Lane c1910 (W.Y.)*

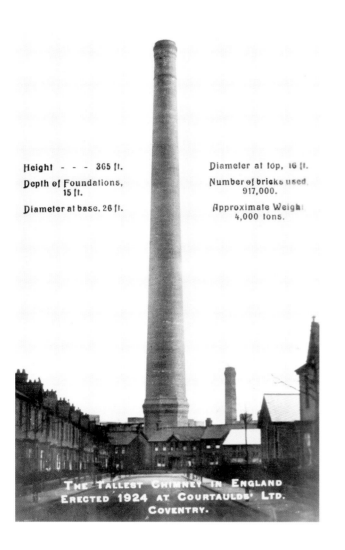

Height - - - 365 ft.

Depth of Foundations, 15 ft.

Diameter at base, 26 ft.

Diameter at top, 16 ft.

Number of bricks used, 917,000.

Approximate Weight 4,000 tons.

THE TALLEST CHIMNEY IN ENGLAND ERECTED 1924 AT COURTAULDS' LTD. COVENTRY.

Courtaulds was as much a part of the technological revolution that hit Coventry this century as the motor firms. The factory was opened in July 1905 to produce the new "artificial silk" developed and refined in various inventors' labs in the previous decade. It was not developed well enough, however, and the company struggled initially, but by the time the picture below was taken the company had sorted out the problems. So well had they succeeded where other larger companies in other countries had failed, that they were able to establish themselves among the world leaders in artificial fibre production. Such large scale expansion meant that much of the original buildings shown were swept away in an series of expansions from the First World War onwards. Included in this development was the Courtaulds chimney, now demolished, behind the junction of Guild Road and Pridmore Road. Courtaulds business has now closed after a period of decline and the site is slowly being cleared. The main central factory has been carefully preserved and converted into offices.

*Courtaulds, Foleshill Road, c1910 (Waterman)*

*Unveiling the Foleshill Memorial, Lockhurst Lane 1919 (Sylvester)*

These two postcards give a panoramic view of the early stages in the life of the Great Heath estate as well as an important occasion for the locals. The event is the unveiling of the Foleshill War Memorial on the 21st September 1919. It had been presented by Mr W. T. Henderson, a local businessman. The view above shows Lockhurst Lane to the left, with the roof of Foleshill railway station clearly showing beside it. The hoarding proclaims the construction of the Great Heath estate. Development is by the ubiquitous Newcome Estates, to be found throughout twentieth century Coventry wherever there was land to be built on. In the centre of the picture is the name Durbar Avenue, unadopted. This partially developed street can be seen on the other view (below). The memorial was only made of wood and plaster, its conversion into stone did not take place. Its location was just outside the Railway Hotel in a spot that has become an isolated backwater with the later construction of a road bridge over the railway line.

*Unveiling the Foleshill Memorial, Durbar Avenue 1919 (Sylvester)*

*Foleshill Station Foot Bridge, Lockhurst Lane c1925 (Unknown)*

These two views tell the tale of early traffic congestion in Coventry and its solution. The development of factories in Foleshill during the First World War led to massive holdups at the level crossing in Lockhurst Lane. It took fifteen years for a real solution to be found. In the meantime the original Railway Hotel was demolished in 1922 to make way for the present larger building that could more easily handle the extra custom in the area. A footbridge was built but that did not ease the road traffic problem. It was only in 1931 that a bridge was built to carry traffic over the railway at a cost of £50,000. As can be seen in the second picture, shop owners on Lockhurst Lane were compensated by rebuilding their frontage up to the level of the new bridge. There have been few other changes over the years, though the appearance of the buildings has deteriorated somewhat.

New Bridge, Lockhurst Lane, Foleshill, Coventry.

*New Bridge, Lockhurst Lane c1931 (Teesee)*

*Grand Theatre, Foleshill Road c1925 (Teesee)*

The Grand Theatre is not so grand any more, the wonderful facade of this cinema is now represented by a triangle of rendered concrete over a dry cleaning shop. The cinema was more or less opposite Homesdale Road, where the spired building can be seen on the right. Its spires are now missing, but there is still a large stone on the gable dating its construction to 1908. The cinema was built later in 1911.

*Shops and St Paul's Church, Foleshill Road c1912 (Waterman)*

This set of shops at the junction with Webster Road have been replaced today with a Co-op store. The host of detail in the notices around the shop windows suggest there was little that the modern store supplies which could not be met by these traders. There is also a sign advertising the nearby Foleshill Palace cinema (see above). The church of St Paul's can be seen in background with its original tower, built in 1841. The church was rebuilt after being substantially damaged by bombing in 1940.

*Holmesdale Road, Foleshill c1912 (Waterman)*

Seemingly greatly changed today, on closer inspection not that much is substantially different. But parked cars crowd the street where garish yellow lines do not intrude and the neatness of uniform frontages is missing. Like all other streets of this period the ornate ironwork has now disappeared as a result of the campaign to collect scrap metal for the Second World War. The neighbourhood police station on the left no longer exists, and a car park stands in its place.

*The General Wolfe, Foleshill Road c1925 (Teesee)*

As one of the most famous landmarks on the Foleshill Road the General Wolfe has worn the century well. Though having lost few of its original architectural details, many of the buildings around it have suffered more severe changes including the demolition of the original Edwardian shops seen here alongside the pub. While the road today has lost its old clutter of tram wires and rails, the modern clutter of street furniture is a necessary if much worse blight on the district.

*Stoney Stanton Road c1905 (Unknown)*

This rather grand view of Stoney Stanton Road shows the dead straight line of a road constructed in 1774 when the lands of the area were enclosed. In 1830 it was turnpiked, an indication of its development as one of Coventry's main radial routes. Originally known as Leicester New Road or Red House Road, it grew in importance in the latter part of the last century by serving one of the few areas where unrestricted industrial development could take place. The scene here clearly shows the line of the tram route to the Bell Green terminus with a tram coming away from town up the slope to Priestley's Bridge. On the left is the Co-op Society's grocery and drapery departments.

*Coventry and Warwickshire Hospital, Stoney Stanton Road c1938 (Teesee)*

Today little remains of the Coventry and Warwickshire Hospital and that that does is quite different to the neat original built in the mid 1860s. It was constructed in the fashionable gothic style on just two acres at the beginning of the Stoney Stanton Road. The 60 bed accommodation was quite enough for Coventry's needs, but the expansion of the city consequently led to the expansion of the hospital, quite swamping the original building, seen here to the left. Bombing during the war put paid to what was left. The opening of the new super hospital at Walsgrave in 2006 meant the removal of most facilities from the city centre and the demolition of the buildings.

*The Ordnance Works, Ordnance Road c1908 (Unknown)*

Though a factory had been operating on the site for a decade or so beforehand, it only became officially the Coventry Ordnance Works in 1906. Metal tubes for bicycles then became barrels for guns. The area occupied by the works shown above rapidly expanded to surround Smith Street, off Red Lane, and was only constrained by the barrier of the Coventry canal. During the First World War traffic on the Stoney Stanton Road would be frequently stopped by a train from the works, shown below, carrying massive naval guns from the numerous factory sidings to the main Coventry to Nuneaton line. In the second view one of the first large guns from the ordnance is shown being transported in June 1912. The photographer is standing on Priestley's Bridge looking out of town with the Ordnance Works to the right and Webster's Brick Works on the left.

*Gun Barrel Crossing, Stoney Stanton Road c1912 (T-H Co)*

*Bell Green Road c1939 (Richards)*

Though comparatively recent views, these pictures of Bell Green both illustrate how important trams were to pre-war life in Coventry. The rails in the road, the wires above it and the clanking of the vehicles themselves were a common experience for those living along their route. While sights such as the man changing over the pickups on trams at Bell Green terminus, below, may be gone, the buildings remain substantially the same. This is more than can be said for the buildings shown in the Bell Green Road view above which have been demolished to improve the flow of modern traffic.

*Tram Terminus, Bell Green c1939 (Richards)*

*Hall Green Road, Bell Green c1906 (E.R.)*

The presence of the Rose and Crown on the right of the picture gives away the location of this view. There is absolutely nothing else to suggest its present location at the junction of Hall Green Road and Bell Green Road. The pub has been replaced with modern building on the same site, but set back from the road. Needless to say, one of Coventry's rare thatched cottages on the left no longer exists.

*Old Church Lane, Bell Green c1906 (E.R.)*

To the keen eye there remain clear similarities between this view and the way it looks today, but it is the detail of the scene that disguises those similarities. Today the road is made up with clearly defined pavements and the houses have painted rendering hiding the characteristic brickwork. Water butts do not catch the rain water from the guttering nor do children play in the road. Newer housing fills in the gaps. Looking towards Bell Green, the house on the left is opposite the Non-Conformist Chapel, with the more modern instrusion of Pearson Avenue a hundred yards or so on the left.

*Hawkesbury Church, Lenton's Lane c1925 (Teesee)*

St Matthew's Mission Church was originally a corrugated iron building built in 1895 but had been given a concrete facing by the time this picture was taken. This rather quaint construction only just outlived its centenary year, being closed in disrepair in 1963. With the school and pub it provided a focus for the area of Hawkesbury of which only The Old Crown survives. The land immediately behind the pub on which the church once stood has now been used for housing.

*Tusse's Bridge, Hawkesbury Lane c1925 (Teesee)*

A charming canalside pub on a quiet country road would be greatly valued today, that is if it were not for the road widening and bridge building over the years that has raised what is now a fairly busy suburban road to the height of the roof of the Elephant and Castle. This little area grew up around servicing the needs of the canal but has suffered badly from twentieth century developments, not least of which is the elevated M6 only a few yards away.

Coventry's first nineteenth century planned suburban development began in Hillfields in 1828 and consequently by the turn of the century had little left of the old rural area except Primrose Hill House, a building of indeterminate age. That does not mean to say that there was no heritage worth preserving – quite the contrary. This became Coventry's premier ribbon weaving area with many houses operating their own weaving looms. But more particularly there was the Vernon Street triangle, Hillfields own rather special contribution to the Industrial Revolution, where the factory system was combined with the workers domestic residence.

It is not perhaps the sort of working operation we would want to see today but its imaginative preservation along with much else, now missing, could have avoided the alienation that the tower block substitutes bring. Modernisation schemes like that found in Winchester Street and Colchester Street provide much better solutions to housing problems than wholesale redevelopment and the consequent destruction of community spirit.

*Victoria Street c1926 (G. & Co)*

This busy street at the heart of Hillfields was an important shopping centre on a main tram route from town to Stoke. It was part of mainstream Coventry and not so much the marginalised community that it is today. It still has a number of small shops serving the needs of the local area but no longer attracting those from further afield. Though there have been many changes to the frontages over the years this view into town is still recognisable from the roof tops and in particular from the top shops that still survive. Adelade Street is just to the right.

*Primrose Hill Park, Payne's Lane c1913 (Waterman)*

This was one of Coventry's first suburban parks. The expansion of Stoke had deprived the Hillfields area of ready access to the natural park of the countryside, which by this date had been pushed back to Clay Lane. The location of the park is the old garden of Primrose Hill House which was the only building in this area at the start of the nineteenth century. The house itself was demolished in 1913 and public baths built in its place. All that remains of the old estate is the lodge house shown in the foreground here but since demolished. The uneveness of the ground in the park is a result of old medieval quarry workings.

*Payne's Lane c1925 (Teesee)*

This particular corner, at the junction of Paynes Lane and Walsgrave Road, has provided interesting shopping attractions for most of the last century until it was submerged under the Sky Blue Way in the late 1980s. It is unrecognisable today although Lloyds Bank on the opposite corner remains.

# KERESLEY

Keresley shares much of its history with Coundon, as it did its church, but the past 150 years have created some rather peculiar internal changes of their own. For centuries Keresley was a village of two halves, Keresley Green to the north and Keresley Heath to the south. The former was of the greatest antiquity but the latter became the most prosperous and it was at Keresley Heath that the church and schools were built in the last century. Then in 1911 a colliery was built near Keresley Green and the centre of prosperity moved northwards. Boundary changes and the expansion of suburban Coventry maintained the split character of the area until in 1974 Keresley was reunited within the boundary of Coventry.

The original rural nature is still evident in some of the western parts of the district but the steady expansion of housing and the creation of a large industrial estate on the site of the Colliery/ Homefire Plant mean it is very much another suburb of Coventry. The suburban character of this area will be reinforced even more if the plans for many new homes on greenfield sites in the village come to fruition.

*Old School, Tamworth Road c1913 (Mills)*

Despite its name and ancient appearance the school was not so very old, having been erected in 1852 at the junction of New Road and Tamworth Road to accommodate the demands of a growing village. Initially it consisted of just the tower and wing which was made up of two classrooms on the first floor and a flat below. Later, in 1875, an extension was built, made up of an additional classroom upstairs and extra space downstairs which was eventually used as the schoolmaster's house. Needless to say the building no longer exists, being demolished in 1962 some time after its closure in 1944. A bland block of flats has replaced it.

*Akon House, Sandpits Lane c1905 (Sidwell)*

Located near the Bennett's Road end of Sandy Lane, this is one of the oldest houses in the area. It had probably performed its original function, as a farmhouse, for at least 350 years. During this century up to the Second World War, the house was the centre of the Sanders Dairy business (note the butter wagon). It was also known locally for its tea gardens. However, with its farmland becoming detached from the house, it was only its listed status and the action of the city council which has preserved it, though its present setting in the middle of a hotel is not the best backdrop to appreciate it.

*Bennett's Road South, Keresley Heath c1905 (Sidwell)*

A rather bleak view, but one that is typical of the piecemeal housing development that was going on in Coventry's northern parishes before the First World War. The view is looking north to Keresley Green along Bennett's Road South. Immediately to the left is New Road with The Bell pub just hidden in the distance. Both sets of terraced housing to the left and right were of comparatively recent construction, the one of these on the left also serving as a shop.

*Aerial view of Coventry Colliery 1939 (The Aerial Photographic Company)*

The opening up of the pit at Keresley in 1911 obviously had an important impact on the community both in terms of the physical presence of the pit and the influx of miners, their families and the associated housing. Although the houses remain the pit has now closed as has the notorious Homefire Plant built alongside it in the 1960s. At least less pollution is produced by the huge Prologis Business Park that is now on the site.

*Bennett's Road, Keresley Green c1925 (Valentines)*

The preservation of the mature trees which lined the road before the houses were built give a pleasant aspect to this rather simply built colliery village, certainly little enough money was spent on the external appearance of the buildings. Unfortunately Keresley End Post Office has closed and the shop gone, though the trees remain. Little has been done to improve the general appearance of the area as time has passed, though home ownership is changing the face of some buildings.

# LONGFORD

Though officially part of Foleshill, Longford has retained a distinctive identity that marks it out from the other hamlets that make up Foleshill. Its location part way between the coal mines of Bedworth and the city of Coventry with the road, rail and canal links passing through it, made it a natural place for early industrial development. It was the main centre of upper Foleshill and with brickworks, gas works, electricity power station and the Coventry Fat and Bone Company established in the area by the early twentieth century, Longford was probably not the most pleasant of environments in which to live!

However, there is a remarkable amount of the physical fabric of this community that has survived the changes of the last two hundred years giving it sense of continuity that most other areas of Coventry have lost. Certain parts of this district, if located elsewhere in Coventry, would have been preserved years ago. It is to be hoped that the same benefits that have preserved the best of Allesley can be applied to Longford.

*Longford Station, Woodshires Road c1913 (Waterman)*

This service to the people of Longford and Exhall closed in 1949 one year short of its centenary. However, the Coventry and Nuneaton line had not been opened with passenger traffic uppermost in mind. The many collieries and brickworks in the vicinity guaranteed its success and contributed to the decline of the canal. The chimney of one of these concerns, The Foleshill Brick and Tile Company, founded in 1897, can be seen in the picture. A few signs of its location just above the Woodshires Road bridge can still be seen today. It is possible that a station might open again nearby to serve the needs of traffic to the Ricoh Arena.

*Longford Road c1913 (Waterman)*

With this view towards Bedworth (above) of the blacksmith shoeing a horse on the immediate left, and ivy covered cottages beyond, a case could be made for village style existence in Longford. However, if the Coventry to Bedworth tram service did not destroy this illusion then the coming of electricity, as can be seen on the right, would soon end any feeling of isolation. The same electricity installation works can be seen on the left of the lower picture. This photograph was taken from the same spot (the canal bridge) and at the same time as the previous one, but this time looking towards Coventry. The scene has not changed that much today, a tribute to the living history of Longford that deserves wider recognition and preservation. Some of the shopfronts alone are worthy of a visit.

*Bedworth Road c1913 (Waterman)*

*Salem Baptist Chapel, Lady Lane c1913 (Waterman)*

Though still standing in its rather out of the way location behind Longford Square, being isolated could result in this attractive chapel being either altered or demolished without being noticed. It signifies more than 200 years of non-conformist worship in this area. Having been through a number of rebuilds since its original construction in 1765, the present frontage dates from 1872. The churchyard alone can be appreciated for offering an oasis of rural peace in this built-up area.

*Aerial view of Gas Works, Rowley's Green c1925 (Unknown)*

By the early part of the twentieth century demand for gas had so outstripped the capacity of the 4.5 acre site in Gas Street, Radford that an urgent search for a larger site led to the move to Rowley's Green. The view shown is an artist's impression superimposed on an aerial photograph. Longford Road crosses the top of the picture with the Windmill Road junction in the centre. Since the first edition of this book the redevelopment of this site has seen the construction of the Ricoh Arena to the right of the gas holder with the Tesco retail park taking up much of the space between the railway line in the foreground and the canal snaking across the middle.

# RADFORD

The changes in Radford brought about by the twentieth century expansion of Coventry are perhaps more remarkable than those found in any other area of the city. Before the First World War it was just another sleepy hamlet around the church of St. Nicholas; admittedly industry and housing were encroaching on its borders with Foleshill in the east and the city centre in the south, but life elsewhere was essentially rural.

It was protected from substantial development by the lack of adequate sewerage facilities, yet once this was overcome there was no stopping the builders and by the time the Second World War broke out there was virtually no land left to build on. What makes Radford's case particularly sad is the fact that today there is next to nothing left of the old settlement except the images preserved in old photographs.

*Radford Road c1913 (Mills later published by T-H Co)*

Here is the calm before the storm. The writing is on the wall, or rather the sign, which advertises the services of Ernest Twigg, builder, who is offering to build homes on the land to the left hand side of the road. The site is at the southern entrance to the village just before the church. Soon a street known as Dugdale Road will be built here. The large house to the right, behind the wall, will survive a little longer. It was known as The Spring, named after the natural spring that can just be seen where it rises, set into the wall, a few feet up from the bench on the right hand side. By the late 1930s the Savoy cinema had taken over the site and though it continues as a bingo hall and social club, the present building does not reflect its earlier glory.

*Radford Church, Radford Road c1913 (Mills later published by T-H Co)*

Though many air raids afflicted Coventry in the early years of the Second World War, St. Nicholas's fate was to be hit by a land mine on the night of the most notorious raid of all, the Coventry Blitz, 14th November 1940. The explosion was also responsible for the deaths of four local people. The church destroyed in the raid was consecrated in 1874 almost ten years after building had started. Although a new church was built nearby in the 1950s, the old churchyard remains, but without a trace of the church.

*The Common, Radford c1913 (Mills later published by T-H Co)*

Unusually, this is a reminder of lost terraced housing not rural views. All the houses shown survived beyond the Second World War, with the junction of Beake Avenue substituting the garden wall on the right and the Engleton Road junction created to the left. Radford Common however was saved. Originally part of common land that stretched as far as Hearsall Common as late as the 1850s, by 1913 there was barely 4.5 acres left. In 1927 the council preserved the lot as a recreation ground for everyone to use.

*Radford Road c1907 (Slapoffski)*

Although separated by a decade, these two views illustrate clearly the march of progress affecting Radford. The first general view, above, shows an essentially rural scene with fields surrounding the school to the left and the 'Grapes Inn' on the right. The church can be seen in isolation on the far left. In the second picture, taken just outside the school to the left, the road is neatly kerbed on both sides and lamp posts have been erected. The first stage of the new Radford estate, mentioned earlier, has been constructed just beyond the school where telegraph poles also make an appearance. Today, these 'new' houses, opposite Joseph's Avenue, later known as Lydgate Road, are all that is left of both of these views.

*Radford Road c1914 (Coupon Photo Co)*

*Barrs Hill School, Radford Road c1910 (Waterman)*

The vocal, ultimately unsuccessful campaign to save the original building on which Barrs Hill School was based was one of the more prominent cries from the heart of Coventry people. It was built in the 1850s and last occupied privately by J. K. Starley, inventor of the Rover Safety Bicycle. In 1908 it became Coventry's first secondary school for girls not long before this picture was taken. Although still a school today, by the early 1980s the cost of repairing what had been the main residence was no longer considered justifiable given changing educational needs. Unfortunately planners forget that a link with the past is often what students need to give them greater encouragement when they feel part of a long tradition.

*St Nicholas Vicarage, St Nicholas Street c1924 (Teesee)*

This house built as a Vicarage in 1837 on the site of the ancient church of St Nicholas, became as can be seen, the premises of H. H. Thompson. This company who moved from their premises in High Street, in 1918, when they purchased the old Vicarage in St Nicholas Close, were the producers of a vast number of local postcards. The premises were unfortunately destroyed in the Blitz. According to Dugdale the original St Nicholas was the first church built in the city which would make this one of the most historic sites in the city.

*Radford Road c1923 (Ralph's Real Photos)*

None of these buildings exist today, not even a modern version of the 'Buck and Crown', just to the left of the second telegraph pole. Today a petrol station dominates where the nearest set of buildings were, while the second set of buildings have been demolished to leave open land just before the junction of Engleton Road and Radford Road. Only a slope in the path and a set of railings, to match the position of those in the picture, gives away its location today.

*Buck and Crown, Radford Road c1910 (Unknown)*

This view taken looking in the opposite direction from the picture above shows the 'Buck and Crown' with a very narrow Radford Road stretching away towards the city on the left. Although Radford had been encompassed by the 1890 boundary changes to bring it into the city, here it still has that village look about it. The 'Buck and Crown' ceased to be a pub long before these buildings were demolished in the late 1950s.

The writing was on the wall for the rural way of life in Stoke as early as 1856 when streets were laid out in the Stratford Road area. Ten years later, the site for the Stoke Park estate was being established on what had been the city's racecourse. Even here, though, the building of actual houses at these locations was slow until the turn of the century. But in the early twentieth century factories and housing were forcing back the countryside in a much more comprehensive way. Gosford Green, once a gateway to the country, was now firmly within the town.

Further development in the 1920s and 1930s saw the old parish completely swallowed up and the town nudging at Walsgrave, Binley and Willenhall. But Coventry's continued prosperity was based on the expansion of industry such as the Humber, Hillman and Peel-Connor works. The latter especially led urban development well away from the city centre as early as the First World War. The more functional development of mains sewerage in the 1930s was just as important in allowing large scale suburban development.

*Stoke Church, Walsgrave Road c1912 (Waterman)*

Stoke was a strange village, in as much as you would expect to find it clustered around the parish church, but with the exception of a pub and a few cottages, there was little to suggest this was the centre of the settlement. Indeed the area around Stoke Green especially, was far more developed. Today there is only the church left of the original buildings that could be found at the turn of the century. Even that is now enveloped by a sea of suburbia. Certainly this view of the south west side of the church would be impossible to reproduce today as the lower part of Shakespeare Street would be in the way.

*Church Lane c1912 (Waterman)*

The contrast between this view of Stoke with the scene today is quite staggering. It shows a country lane near its junction with the Walsgrave Road. The tall weavers' top shops on the left and the original Rose and Crown pub beyond have gone, as too have the other cottages on the right, opposite the church entrance. New trees have come with the houses, but their regularity seems poor compensation for the picturesque appearance of the ancient hedgerows.

The Rectory had only a short life of less than eighty years. It was built in 1893 by the Reverend T.A. Blythe, writer of the definitive 'History of Stoke'. The traditional home of the ministers of Stoke had been Walsgrave Rectory as they were also responsible for that parish. Their new home, however, was demolished in the 1960s to make way for a block of flats which still exist at the junction of Church Lane with Binley Road.

*Stoke Rectory, Binley Road c1912 (Waterman)*

*Bourne Road c1927 (G. & Co.)*

Apart from the Humber, the next big industrial development in Stoke was the construction of the Conner Magneto & Ignition Works built in 1916. It was then expanded in 1921 as the Peel-Connor Telephone works. It was accompanied by housing for the workers. Later known as the G.E.C., the factory expanded to take over some of these roads; such was the fate of Bourne Road in the 1970s. Since the first edition of this book all work at the factory has ceased.

*Binley Road c1925 (Teesee)*

Much of the story of Coventry's suburbs is that of development rather than redevelopment. This photograph is rare testimony to the latter. The view is that of the old Bull's Head inn to the right and the site of the present Empress Buildings that replaced the buildings to the left. They were described by the Midland Daily Telegraph as "a block of dilapidated property which for many years has been an eyesore" This statement was made in 1933 on the announcement of the construction of Empress Buildings which, when finished was said to leave Binley Road "one of the most picturesque in Coventry". It did not mention the destruction of the 400 year old smithy that was amongst the buildings shown here on the left.

*The Horse Pond, Stoke Green c1912 (Waterman)*

Another postcard of this view describes it as 'Gentlemans Green', possibly dating from the time that Stoke Cricket Club used to play their matches here. However, the pond is what has lodged in people's memories over the years. Commonly known at the time as 'the Horse pond', many a horse and trap would take a diversion through its waters on a hot summers day. While the horse had its fill of water the wooden wheels would swell to tighten on their metal rims. This was very important because the rims might otherwise have fallen off if the wood had contracted too much with the dryness of the day. Within twenty years of the previous view, the once innocent pond has taken a large step into being an integrated part of urban society. From providing a service to horse drawn traffic and the occasional intrepid child, it had become a fully sanitised, stone walled, piped facility for the area's youth. In the last twenty years the pool has been filled in a victim of maintenance costs and health and safety concerns.

*The Bathing Pool, Stoke Green c1933 (Teesee)*

*Gosford Green, Walsgrave Road c1911 (Waterman)*

This view looking towards Stoke was taken before the construction of the Gosford Spur railway line, now the route of the Phoenix Way. The backs of the houses in Kingsway Road and St. Margaret's church can still be seen. The buildings on the left make up Gosford Terrace which contain an interesting mixture of the sacred and the profane; St Joseph's Convent and the White Lion public house, sadly neither is still with us. Both were bombed in the war, with just the pub being rebuilt, only to be demolished by road developments in the late 1980s.

*Ball Hill, Walsgrave Road c1926 (G. & Co.)*

For these children in Ball Hill there was little traffic to worry about while their parents were in Brookes newsagents, or next door in Hailstone's knicker shop. By the 1920s this road was a well established part of suburban Coventry. But only two decades earlier it had been described as being made of loose slag and stone so that it required two horses to pull a cart up Ball Hill.

*Workmen leaving the Humber, Humber Road c1910 (W.Y.)*

The building of the Humber Works a couple of years before this photograph was taken brought about a permanent change to the character of Stoke let alone the sleepy country track known as Folly Lane. The remains of the lane can be seen just beyond the emerging workmen. It had not even been left with the dignity of its old name, though, as late as the 1920s there was disagreement between the City Council who called it Folly Lane and Coventry Rural District who insisted it was Humber Road.

*Gosford Green, Binley Road c1912 (W.Y.)*

Across the park at the end of the line of trees stands the recently erected bridge (but not yet the embankment) belonging to the Gosford Spur railway line, eventually opened in 1914. The park itself is only cultivated in the near corner, together with the new fountain. The rest looks much as it did when Coventry City F.C. played some of its early games here.

*Clements Street c1912 (Waterman)*

Though appearing a rather ordinary street scene, not much different from today, there are many subtle variations which date this view as being from another era. There are no parked cars lining the streets, the roofs are not bristling with TV aerials (let alone satellite dishes) nor do telephone lines criss-cross the sky. The houses still have an architectural unity unchanged by 'Cotswold' stone cladding, painted brickwork, double glazing or any other of the many forms of home improvements that characterize today's terraced streets.

*Stoke Schools, Briton Road c1912 (Waterman)*

The original Stoke School was more of a school serving a village community when it was built in 1876, but its enlargement in 1911, shown here, graphically illustrates the way that the city was forcing its way into the countryside. The extension was to accommodate the rising population of Stoke, but its log book was still recording the trek of pupils over the fields in winter and the temporary enrolment of children of passing gypsies. It was demolished in the 1980s and a new school now occupies the site.

*Walsgrave Road c1934 (Teesee)*

The second wave of urban growth in Stoke came in the early 1930s. This view shows part of the recently constructed Wyken House estate to the right, known today as Poets Corner. Wyken House itself was demolished at this time and little remains except a few outbuildings behind the shops half way down Longfellow Road.  In 1934 the Forum cinema was built with seating for 1,570 people. It must have made quite an impression with its bright clean concrete façade; however, on its demolition in 1962 it looked a shadow of its former self. The Forum Bowling Alley that replaced it has also closed recently with planning permission to be converted into a church. The contrasting uses of this site in the years since it was occupied by the picturesque lodge to Wyken House, which originally occupied this spot, could not be greater.

*Forum Cinema, Walsgrave Road 1934 (Teesee)*

# STYVECHALL, CANLEY AND TILE HILL

These three Coventry suburbs were amongst the last to be fully developed in the twentieth century. They cover most of the southern boundary of the city. Until the 1930s they had no significant residential or industrial incursions, excepting that of the Standard Works built at Canley during the First World War. The reasons for their long reprieve and the subsequent shape of their development, was a combination of the conservatism of the landed gentry and the foresight of the city council.

Styvechall, was in the hands of the Gregory family since the sixteenth century and remained a rural parish on the edge of the city centre until the start of the 1920s when the War Memorial Park was laid out. Improved access to all three areas was affected with the construction of the Coventry by-pass in the mid to late 1930s, which provided the necessary stimulus to various building schemes. Styvechall hamlet was preserved thanks to a gift to the city by the owners in 1932. Fortunately, Styvechall Common, Canley Ford, the avenue on Kenilworth Road, and various woodland in the Tile Hill area, were also preserved by the purchase of 200 acres of land from Lord Leigh of Stoneleigh by the City Council. Knowing that planning regulations were very loose in those days this was the only way that the Council felt they could control development and preserve significant rural features. The foresight of the council has certainly been to the overall benefit of the ratepayers over the years.

*The Grove and Memorial Park, Kenilworth Road c1923 (HHT Premier)*

Although it would be a while longer before the Memorial Park gates would be erected, this picture taken after the Park was officially opened in 1921, indicates how quickly it had become a popular leisure area. It would also appear, by the admiring glances the two girls are receiving from the boys that this was, like the 'Bunny Run', a good courting spot.

*The Grove and Toll House, Warwick Road c1914 (Unknown)*

Two gates and fencing would have originally prevented other than pedestrians using the roads seen above, unless a toll of 6d/vehicle, 1d/horse was paid. The gate on the left across the road to Styvechall, Baginton and Stoneleigh (now Leamington Road) the other across the road to Kenilworth and Warwick. The toll received permitted the Gregory Family who owned the Toll House, to repair the roads which passed across their land. In 1919, when Coventry Corporation purchased the land on which the Memorial Park was to be built, certain cottages and the Toll House were included in the sale. To permit the road to be widened when the park was laid out, the entrance to the house was moved from the front (lower picture) to the side. Although traffic lights were erected at this junction, the road was not further widened, but even so, amid a storm of protest, the Toll House, built in 1812 was demolished in 1964. As all of the cars in the lower picture are Rovers it could be that the occasion was a works outing to Stratford-upon-Avon or the Cotswolds.

*The Toll House, Warwick Road c1907 (Jackson)*

*Styvechall Common, Earlsdon Avenue South c1912 (Mills)*

Taken at a time when children could happily play on their own, this view shows them on Styvechall Common, with a very narrow Earlsdon Avenue South in the background. Kenilworth Road and the area to become the Memorial Park is just to the right of the picture. The girls on the footpath, are cutting through from Kenilworth Road on their way down into Earlsdon, to the left.

*Coat of Arms Bridge, Coat of Arms Bridge Road c1912 (Waterman)*

When in 1840 a proposal was made to build a railway branch line from Coventry to Leamington, land owners and farmers including Mr. A. F. Gregory passed a resolution to oppose this. In 1842 he agreed to sell sufficient land to enable the railway to go ahead on condition that his family coat of arms be incorporated on the new bridge, which was eventually built in 1844. The amount of traffic now using this route, would not allow such a casual stroll down the edge of the road.

*Kenilworth Road c1910 (Harvey Barton)*

Kenilworth Road always has been one of the most beautiful roads into the city, particularly as a result of the planting of the avenue of oaks in the eighteenth century. Even before the Memorial Park was opened this area gave much pleasure to Coventry workers in their free time. A walk out to Kenilworth on Sunday was popular, one of the treats on the journey obviously being to buy a 'Codd' bottle of Ginger Beer or a banana from this street seller. As she is standing near to Earlsdon Avenue South, she may have pushed her wicker cart to this spot from Earlsdon.

*Kenpas Highway Crossing c1938 (Teesee)*

This view looking towards the city shows the newly completed section of the Coventry by-pass where it crossed the Kenilworth Road, with Kenpas Highway to the right. If this by-pass, planned as early as the mid nineteenth century, had been built sooner it could have eased the redevelopment of the centre of Coventry. It was the volume of traffic from Birmingham to London, which had to pass right through the centre of the city which created the need for more and wider roads. The quality of street furniture, especially the lighting is worthy of note.

*Earlsdon Avenue North c1925 ("The Three Spires" series, G. & Co.)*

Until the boundary changes in 1928, the terminus of this Maudslay Corporation bus was Hearsall Common, where passengers could quench their thirst at the combined drinking fountain and horse trough. This was erected in 1920 by employees of the Coventry Chain Co., in memory of their 45 comrades who fell in the First World War. Although not damaged, this attractive monument was taken down after the Second World War and later re-erected by Spon End Arches where the old Coventry Chain factory stood. The common is shown still fenced from the days when Freemen of the City could graze animals on the land. The Clarence public house, now The Old Clarence can be seen in the background.

*Beechwood Avenue and Canley Road, Hearsall Common c1913 (Waterman)*

Like other commons on the edge of the city, Hearsall Common in Victorian times had been used for the dumping of domestic rubbish, but by 1894 had been laid out as a nine hole golf course for Hearsall Golf Club until moving to its present site in 1911. At the time of this postcard the Standard Motor Co. had not yet been built by Canley railway station to the right. Over the railway bridge what was to become Beechwood Avenue was still known as Whor Lane. The cottages seen on the right were demolished soon after this picture was taken. The Farmhouse pub now occupies this site.

*Level Crossing, Canley Road c1925 (Teesee)*

The men seen cycling over the crossing could well have just left the Standard Motor Works, as the entrance into the factory is further down on the left. This factory, opened in 1915 to manufacture aeroplanes in large numbers during the First World War, had grown to cover over 10 acres of floor area by 1925. The main office block, known as Ivy Cottage can be seen just to the left of the street lamp. Canley Gates Farm which can be seen just to the right of the water tower was soon to be demolished. The level crossing itself has now been blocked off and the traffic re-directed through the large retail and business park that now occupies the old factory site.

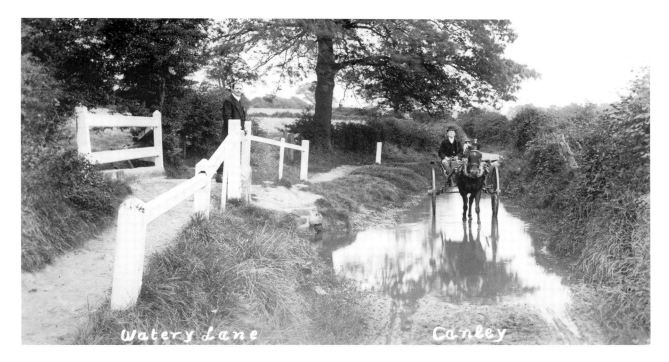

*Watery Lane, Canley c1910 (Unknown)*

Long before the building of the Fletchhamstead Highway, the route from Coventry and Styvechall to Canley would be across Styvechall Common through Canley Ford and Watery Lane. In later years Canley Ford was to become a popular play area for children, who could buy an ice-cream or a milk shake from Canley Milk Bar. Still a popular walk, the Highway end has been spoilt by the building of a garage on the site of the Cedars Cafe. Fortunately today this area is managed by the 'Friends of Canley Ford' who keep an eye on its up-keep.

*Tile Hill Crossroads c1913 (Appleby)*

This view is taken from Banner Lane looking towards Station Avenue and shows the local postman with his delivery bicycle, outside the Post Office Stores to the left. Thatched ricks can be seen in the field to the right, now the site of the HSBC Bank. The delivery carts and girls cycling towards the crossroads are outside the Bell Inn. The finger post on the godcake indicates Coventry four miles to the left with Berkswell Village to the right.

*Post Office Stores, Station Avenue c1930 (Unknown)*

With the exception of the Bell Inn on the opposite side of Station Avenue and Viners Garage to the left of the post office, on the corner of Tile Hill Lane, this store appears to cater for the total needs of the village. In addition to a telephone it is licenced to sell tobacco and cigars together with everything from Carters Tested Seeds to lawnmowers. In later years the building on the right was a cafe. Mr. H. A. Smith the postmaster and storekeeper is shown in the doorway.

*The Bell Inn, Station Avenue c1907 Sidwell)*

Along with the Peeping Tom at Burton Green, this inn served a large community and with Tile Hill railway station a short distance up Station Avenue to the left the Bell would also be a first or last place of call for passengers. The inn is hardly recognisable today having been greatly altered over the years.

*Tanners Lane c1930 (Unknown)*

Here is a very rural view looking from Tanners Lane towards the Banner Lane crossroads, with Tile Hill Lane stretching up the hill in the distance. Tanners Lane was named after Tanyard Farm, the roof of which can just be seen to the left. This timber framed farm was one of the earliest tanneries in the area, and was demolished in 1975 with Tanyard Estate being built on the site soon afterwards. At least the historic value of the farm was appreciated elsewhere as it was later re-erected at Milton Keynes.

*Blacksmith's Shop, Duggins Lane c1930 (Unknown)*

George Duggins senior, father of the last blacksmith, is seen outside his premises, when still in use. The view is looking towards Station Avenue with Conway Avenue, unadopted at the time, being on the left by the lamp post. When the last blacksmith retired, a promise was made to fully restore the premises which has been kept and the building is now a private house.

*Tile Hill Station, Station Avenue c1930 (Teesee)*

This view is from Cromwell Lane looking towards Station Avenue and Tile Hill village, shows the signal box in its original position on the Birmingham side of the crossing. At that time the booking office and Coventry platform was on the opposite side. Later both platforms were on the same Birmingham side and a new signal box was built on the Coventry side. The twenty first century has seen the road converted into a flyover, which is more convenient but feels a little out of place in this semi rural suburb.

How much can be said to be left of the community spirit that was once so apparent in this village? What was the village is now decidedly part of the larger community of Coventry, but it was not always so. In 1927 when proposals were being put forward for Walsgrave to be incorporated within the city boundary, it was stated that there was "no community of interest between it and the city". Walsgrave was a sizeable village with a self contained identity based on its two main sources of employment, mining and agriculture. However, the closure of the village pit and the expansion of housing soon ended such isolation and the road development schemes of the 1960s ripped out what heart there was left in the village centre.

Though there is little romance in having a coal mine on your doorstep, the centre of the village did present an aspect that once rivalled that of Allesley. Though there were not many individual buildings of great historical or architectural importance, together they made up a village community that reflected many centuries of its 1000 year old life. It is a loss that should be condemned every bit as much as if Allesley were bulldozed tomorrow - a village also on a busy road but one fortunate enough to be saved by a by-pass and a conservation order.

*Woodway Lane, c1906 (E.R.)*

This view gives a good impression of the real village of Walsgrave of which a mere skeleton is left today. Only one building, in the centre left of the picture, remained at the time of the first edition of this book. It was known most recently as Ivy Cottage and was by the entrance to Woodway Lane from the Hinkley Road, by the side of a non-descript shop. At the time of the first edition of this book it had been boarded up for years looking ripe for demolition. This was duly carried out a decade later.

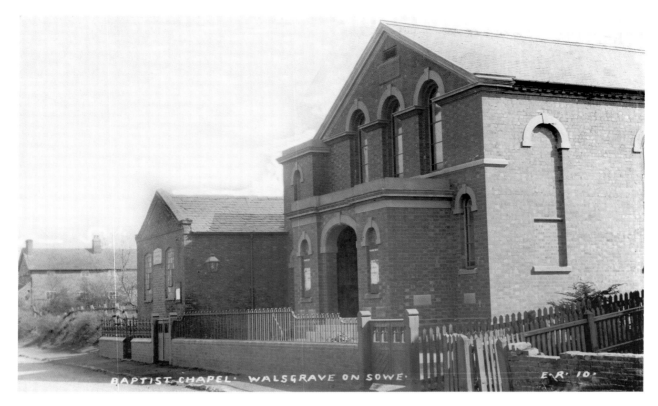

*Baptist Chapel, Hinkley Road c1906 (E.R.)*

There are three stages to the life of Walsgrave Baptist Church. The building on the left is the original one erected in 1840. The enlarged one on the right was constructed in 1901 and was therefore comparatively new when this picture was taken. In the late 1980s yet another addition had been made but unlike the fate of most other parts of Walsgrave it has been done quite thoughtfully and with sympathy to the architecture that preceded it. The original 1840 building no longer exists, being demolished at some stage and replaced by a hall to serve the needs of the chapel.

*Holly Bank, Woodway Lane, c1910 (Unknown)*

To Walsgrave people alive in the first half of this century this house will always be remembered as the home of the Verrall sisters, a formidable pair of spinsters who were very influential in village life for much of the time until their deaths in 1953. The house was located very near the main road end of Woodway Lane until the 1950s, its grounds stretching to the Sowe. Part of what was the garden is now occupied by Beckbury Road.

*Walsgrave War Memorial, Walsgrave Crossroads c1925 (Unknown)*

Some elements of this scene are just as easily identified today as when this photo was taken, soon after the erection of the War Memorial in 1922. The villagers had been sufficiently moved by the loss of fifteen of their community in the 1914-1918 War to raise £300 to cover the cost. Sadly the scene is not so tranquil today; with the church at our back, the view up the Hinckley Road is that of a roaring dual carriageway, not the winding, cottage-lined country lane to be seen on the left of the picture. Only the shop and the memorial remain.

*Walsgrave Hall c1907 (Unknown)*

£15,000 was paid for Walsgrave Hall in 1961 so that it could be demolished and flats built in its place. It's grounds were located on the site of the present Walsgrave hospital but the Hall itself occupied the area known today as Cloister Croft. Evidence suggests that a Hall had existed on this site in one form or another since, at least 1569. Although in its most recent form it was probably less than a couple of centuries old. Its loss was one more nail in the coffin of Walsgrave's old character.

# WHITLEY AND WILLENHALL

It is difficult to imagine how these areas of Coventry were regarded at the turn of the century. Both had a reasonably clear identity but this would appear to be based on the grand homes of their respective principal inhabitants; 'Whitley Abbey' and 'The Chase'. Normal centres of activity such as the pub, the school or the church were missing in either one or the other or both. Neither had suffered particularly from the Edwardian expansion of Coventry and the early 1920s were not much different from earlier decades.

The inter-war years, however, saw the sale and dereliction of Whitley Abbey, the conversion of The Chase into a hotel and the widening of the London Road. This latter act was as sad as any of the changes as it meant the destruction of an avenue of trees providing an entrance to Coventry that rivalled the Kenilworth Road. It is not easy to find saving graces in the changes wrought to this sector of Coventry. It has become the servant of the city with the city doing virtually nothing to preserve any aspect of its original character. Roads, housing, sewage works, hostels, an incinerator, a depot and an airfield have swept away the few links with the past in a more comprehensive way than almost anywhere else in Coventry apart from Radford.

*The Bridge and Old Mill, Abbey Road, Whitley, c1920 (Unknown)*

The new technology passes the old. These Humber cars out on test were very much of the present and future. The mill, however, was out of use by the 1880s and although it continued to be occupied until the early 1950s it was demolished soon after. What does survive is the bridge which carried the old London Road into Coventry. Thomas Telford straightened it in the 19th century to speed stage coaches on their route from London to Holyhead, consequently by-passing (and preserving) this spot. This is the view looking out of Coventry.

*Whitley Abbey from the South, Abbey Road c1906 (Unknown)*

Although Coventry has had more than its fair share of monks through the ages, there has never been a monastic abbey at Whitley. A house has stood on this site since the 14th century but the name Whitley Abbey is a much later invention from the last century. The building in this picture has a seventeenth century core with mainly early 19th century additions. The last family to take up residence was the Petre's in 1867, and it was they who ended its occupation with the sale of the estate in 1924. By the 1950s when the present school was planned for the site only the Roman Catholic chapel was left.

*Whitley Avenue c1906 (Unknown)*

It is difficult to make any connection between this view and its location today, apart from the name. Whitley Avenue was then a private road off Abbey Road leading to four large houses known as Whitley Villas, built in the mid-nineteenth century. In the last twenty years the remaining two have been demolished and replaced by flats and houses. The pillars, shown marking the entrance to the road, have long since disappeared; the road itself is now another part of the 1930s housing estate.

*Whitley Pumping Station, London Road c1907 (Slapoffski)*

This was the original sewage pumping station in Whitley, to the north of the London Road, by the Coventry City Council Depot. The terrace of workers' cottages fronting London Road are now all that is left. Few of the motorists passing the nearby Whitley fly-over would make the connection with this scene today.

*London Road, Whitley c1939 (Richards)*

The reason for the widening of the London Road becomes clear from the scene shown here. Only recently completed, the Whitley Estate has attracted more traffic to the area and commercial through-traffic has become heavier, both in terms of frequency and size. At least our telegraph poles are not quite so prominent today.

*The Seven Stars Inn, London Road, Whitley c1904 (Sidwell)*

This view of the Seven Stars Inn was taken just a short while before its demolition in 1905. It was located near the junction of Abbey Road with the London Road. Its Edwardian replacement still stands, as do some of the original outbuildings (presently home of Folly Lane Old Boys Social Club). The decline of coach travel with the development of the railways had sealed the fate of the building as an inn by the middle of the last century.

*The Chase, London Road, Willenhall c1904 (Sidwell)*

It was not very long after its construction in 1897 that The Chase ceased to be a private residence, but despite its conversion to an hotel by 1930, and subsequent extensions, some of the old character of the house remains. Its first owner, Charles Illife was the City Coroner and Poor Law Doctor and part of the family that established the Coventry Evening Telegraph.

*London Road, Willenhall c1930 (Unknown)*

Despite the increase in street furniture and road markings and the demolition of the cottage in the foreground at the end of the last century, this scene has not changed a great deal. It was the couple of years just before this picture was taken that finished off Willenhall as a quiet hamlet. The widening of Willenhall Bridge and the London Road with the consequent elimination of its avenue of mature trees eased the problems caused by an increasing flow of road traffic.

*St. James' Lane, Willenhall c1904 (Sidwell)*

The cottage on the far left is the same one shown on the far right of the previous picture. Though being one of the oldest cottages in the area and later serving a valuable role in the community as a post office and store. It was demolished, for no apparent reason and has remained an empty plot for twenty years. The old Willenhall Church Mission Rooms built in 1884 can be seen in the middle distance. Subsequently they became the basis of Willenhall Church of England School, still on the site today.

As an area remembered for its coalmines as much as anything else, it seems difficult to decry the building over of Wyken as it has swept the colliery away as well. Furthermore two of the most important buildings of the thirty or so standing in 1900 still survive - the Church and Manor Farm on Henley Road. Yet much of Wyken was open farmland without a nucleated centre. That based around the church disappeared centuries ago, most housing was centred about the various farms.

It was not an area chosen by fashionable Coventry society to build their large houses. However, the scenic aspects it did have were to be rapidly eroded during this century. Initially the odd terrace of colliery housing was built along the Ansty Road followed by the Stoke Heath Estate, created by the Council during the First World War (It was later transferred to Stoke parish). At the outbreak of the Second World War suburbia was within a quarter of a mile of the church and had reached the gates of Caludon Castle.

*Caludon Ruins, Farren Road c1934 (Teesee)*

It is difficult to envisage the importance of Caludon Castle and its inhabitants given the state of the ruins that remain, but it was a building of some substance and its owners, even in the seventeenth century, were of some note. However it was when the house fell into the hands of a parliamentarian that the castle's fate was sealed in the Civil War. The site must have remained habitable for it was only in 1800 that Caludon House was built in the ruins. At this time large parts of the walls were still standing, but today as in the 1930's only one piece is left. At least that is preserved as part of a recreation area where all can appreciate it, which is some advance on the previous seven hundred years.

*Congregational Church, Farren Road, Wyken c1934 (Teesee)*

This is a rare example of community facilities, beyond the strictly commercial, within a 1930's Coventry housing development. As in many of the Coventry housing schemes much of the development of Wyken was engineered by the Newcombe Estate Company who had bought the Wyken House Estate in 1929. As was their practice the land was then sold off to local builders with the infrastructure of roads and drainage all in one place. By 1931, 1,000 homes had been erected in the general area. A plot of land had been secured by the Congregational Church at the junction of Hocking Road and Farren Road to build the Congregational Chapel seen here, opened in 1935. By 1955 a more substantial building had been erected on an adjoining site in Hocking Road.

*Ansty Road, Wyken c1934 (Teesee)*

It seems that the planners showed some foresight in making the Ansty Road a dual carriageway even though the traffic at the time was quite light. It was a decision that would have been difficult to reverse later with the intensive development that the area was experiencing during the 1930's. The view shows the limits of the recently constructed Wyken House Estate on the right near Hipswell Highway on the way out of town.

Nearly all the pictures used in this book were originally postcards. Most often they were contact prints taken from the original glass photographic plate, so in that sense they are first edition photographs. Some were mass-produced in the manner of modern postcards, using a lithographic process. These postcards, though almost of photographic quality, are not as clear as the contact prints. A few used a rather cruder method of taking a line print from an original photograph which produced a less detailed picture, but one that could be coloured. All of them, however, contribute to our understanding of the twentieth century landscape of Coventry. Few of these postcards would have been sent if the government had not decided to halve the postage for postcards from the Id normal letter rate to 1/2d. This fact, together with an, as yet, underdeveloped telephone service meant that the postcard was the cheapest way of keeping in touch. Three or more postal deliveries a day and same day delivery in the cities guaranteed millions of sales of postcards. Cheaper photographic supplies encouraged some amateurs to become professionals and sell views of their area which the larger companies would not bother taking because of the small number of sales involved. We can only guess at their output as few publishers numbered their work in any logical manner and total sales of each postcard view were rarely noted. Certainly the laborious method of hand contact printing would yield a few hundred of each card, at the very most. However, most sales came from niche marketing based on the rarity of the view. So it is to the local photographers that we most often turn for the uncommon view of the side-street or the suburb where the picture of "our area" would tempt the extra penny that such photographic postcards cost. Unlike many towns, Coventry had few photographers with a prolific output before 1912 and after 1918 the boom time was over for the postcard when the government doubled the postage. Unusually therefore, it is easier to use postcards to show changes in Coventry before the First World War than it is for any time since.

### E.R. (EXPRESS PHOTO CO)

Apart from the post war efforts of Thompson & Son no other business so fully recorded the street scenes of Coventry and district. The Express Photo Company was run by Ernest Ratledge who was born in 1880 into a family that made its living from photography in Sheffield. By 1905 he had his own photographic business in Boston, Lincolnshire but by 1906 he was based in Rugby. Although he only stayed in the town for a couple of years he spent his time systematically recording every street and significant building in Coventry (and much of Warwickshire). In doing so he stole a march of at least five years on most other photographers who had yet to move out of the city centre. Considering the pace of development in Coventry at this time, such early visual evidence is invaluable. Sadly the firm was not quite as meticulous in their processing techniques because their sepia postcards are often rather faded. Ratledge's numbering system suggests at least 400 different views were published from within the old city boundary. He continued his technique of employing a canvasser to drum up business from local retailers in other parts of the country until eventually settling down, after the First World War, in Halton in Bedfordshire.

### G. & CO.

A firm whose production from before the First World War until the early thirties filled some important scenic gaps in Coventry's development. The earliest postcards are captioned by hand which makes it appear a one man operation, though the quality of the photographs is often very good. Later cards sometimes described as "The Three Spires" series were much more professionally printed on a larger scale, however, the firm was never a major producer. There are no clues on the cards or in the directories as to the person who ran this business or where it was based.

## JACKSON & SONS

Many Coventry families who had members alive in the city during the latter part of the nineteenth century and the first part of the twentieth century will have studio photographs from Josiah Jackson in their possession. After occupying a couple of studios in Trafalgar Street he settled into premises at 25 Lower Ford Street in 1903 and stayed there for almost twenty years in partnership with his son. Most of their postcards that have survived were of groups and events but they did produce some street scenes. Most of these were produced in larger quantities using a non-photographic printed finish. As you might hope from an experienced professional photographer the standard and composition of the original photographs was consistently high.

## MILLS, A R B

For a small scale, part-time producer of Coventry photographic postcards, Archibald Mills was one the most technically accomplished. An engineer by trade Mills, was living at 7 Northfield Road at the start of his short postcard career in 1911. But when he finished his output around 1914 he was living at 15 Stanley Road, Earlsdon, as noted on the back of some cards. He covered quite a large area of Coventry and Warwickshire, but it his street scenes of Coventry that are particularly well composed, capturing the busy activity in the city centre. His period of postcard production only lasted for these few pre-First World War years, though he continued to do studio photographs after the war. Many of his plates were bought by Coventry High Street Stationers Thompson-Hughes and reprinted under their name, making up the first 100 or so cards of their numbered series. This included most of the most well known views of Earlsdon for this period. Despite being well out of date they continued to be sold into the 1920s.

## RALPH'S REAL PHOTOS

Ralph Athersych came late to postcard photography and was only 19 when he produced his first postcards in 1922. He operated from 5 George Eliot Road, Foleshill for just a few years selling photographic equipment as well as his own postcards. He was not especially prolific but his view cards were well produced and neatly labelled. He seemed to focus particularly on the Radford area and external pictures of local schools. There is no evidence that he covered local events

## RICHARDS, R B & E D

This firm appeared and disappeared in the space of a year, like Ratledge did thirty years earlier. Very little is known about it except its base was in Strensall near York and it covered other urban areas in the Midlands. Its output came at a significant time just before the Second World War when much building work had been done on the outer suburbs of Coventry. It also captured many of the new industrial sites along the southern edge of the city. By 1939, when most of their photographs were taken, Thompson's output had gone into significant decline and so it is to the work of Richards that we turn to see the newly built streets and factories of the period. Many views were captured but few copies of individual views were made and therefore few survive

## SIDWELL OF MERIDEN

The Sidwell name is known locally for the woman who was the Meriden postmistress at the time these postcards were produced. It appears that her husband was the photographer, taking many views of North Warwickshire about the 1904-1907 period. This area coincided with the villages that Arthur Sidwell visited in his role of school attendance officer. This did not include central Coventry, but as an original native of Foleshill he had a small output covering what were to later become city suburbs. Only a few were produced as actual photographs as most used a printing process based on dot prints made up like newspaper photographs. He had an eye for the unusual and some views and buildings can only be found on his postcards.

## H. H. THOMPSON & SON

This was the giant of the Coventry postcard publishing industry, dominating the inter-war period with its creation of new cards of every district of Coventry. Unlike many of the local photographic postcards publishers, Thompson's did not print their own postcards. It is believed that they had them produced in London by Rotary, one of the largest national printers of photographic postcards. In fact they did not even take their own photographs before the 1920s, relying on buying up the plates of other Coventry postcard photographers such as Waterman, Mills and Appleby. They published series of views under a number of names, in order, T-H Co./H.H.T.Cov/H.H.T.Premier Series/Teesee Series. They operated as early as 1909 from a stationer's shop at 30 High Street. In the 1920s they employed a number of reps who would seek out business from local shops in towns and villages in Warwickshire who would order as many as twenty plus different views of their area. They would then send their employees to take the photographs which would be sent to Rotary who would print the cards with the retailer's name on the reverse. Later they even drummed up business from counties far beyond Warwickshire Although the postcard business nationally was declining anyway as the century progressed, the bombing of Thompson's warehouse in St Nicholas Street in the Second World War meant the business could only stagger on for a few years after the war.

## WATERMAN, E T

Edgar Thomas Waterman died in 1924 at the age of 56. As a master stationer he opened a stationery shop at 180 Spon Street in Coventry about 1909 soon after his marriage. He was a Londoner so why he came to Coventry is a mystery. Where his shop was located was originally planned as an off-licence of the 'Rising Sun' pub, and is now back to being part of its lounge. Waterman's homemade postcards were soon a profitable sideline and continued to be for the next five years. For some reason, possibly connected with the First World War, he stopped producing them, though the shop stayed open for another 25 years. A more professional local firm, Thompson-Hughes, later used some of his photographic plates for one of their series of local views. (Mainly the HHT series) Technically the processing and presentation of Waterman's photographs was fairly weak. Often he would get one part of the picture out of focus or get the spellings of his scruffy captioning wrong. Quite a few were also poorly exposed. However, when he was trying he had a good eye for a view composing some original perspectives on otherwise quite common scenes. But why he deserves to be remembered, is for being one of the more prolific postcard photographers of those operating in Coventry in the early part of the century. Although he is best known for his coverage of events such as the Godiva procession of 1911 and the other various processions that were a regular part of the Coventry social scene, his street scenes often captured out of the way places that are of especial value to us today.

## STUDIO BASED PHOTOGRAPHERS

Most photographers referred to in this section did not have studio based businesses where portraiture would be the main source of income. There were though up to seventeen such photographers in Coventry before the First World War. Most did produce some postcards but they tended to be of groups, sports teams and events. Some of there work found its way into the local weekly pictorial news magazine, The Coventry Graphic. A few did also produce the occasional street scene. Most prominent amongst this group of photographers was Ernest Appleby, who had arrived in Coventry in the 1890s to manage the local branch of Maule's photographers. By 1908 he ran the studio at 27 Hertford Street himself. Appleby continued in business throughout the interwar years. Charles Winterbourne worked for a similar period from his studio at 44 Swanswell Terrace. Both produced first class photographs as you might expect from professional photographers. This, however, was not always the case with the work of Blakeman and Saville of 4A Fleet Street and Slias Curtis of 7 Union Street. The former were in business for twenty years from 1901, yet to judge from their poorly finished sepia postcards of street scenes it was just as well that their production was infrequent. Curtis was originally the manager of Sylvester's photographic studio since at least 1911, which he took over on his own account in 1917 (Though a C. Sylvester mysteriously reappeared in charge of the premises in 1921). He advertised in the classified sections of local newspapers for work covering all sorts of family and community events. From the historical record point of view his few years of prolific work are valuable but composition and finish were often disappointingly weak.

A brief index such as this will not be totally comprehensive. Particular attention has been paid to any streets, public buildings, factories, public houses and cinemas featured in the pictures or text.